Shelley Tobisch and Bernie Tobi

ULTIMATE GUIDE TO
Sewing Machine Feet

CHOOSE, USE, AND TROUBLESHOOT YOUR MACHINE FEET FOR SUCCESS

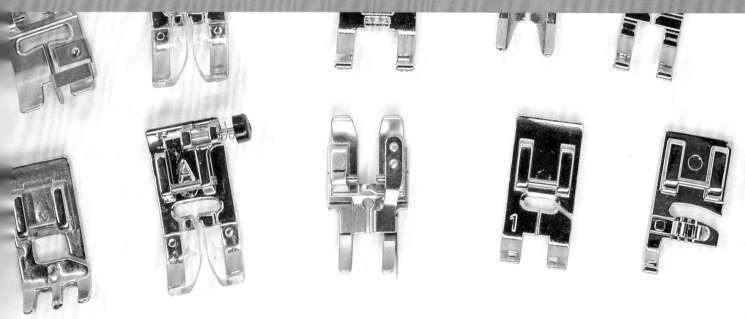

C&T PUBLISHING
Another Maker Inspired!

Text and photography copyright © 2025 by Shelley Marie Tobisch and Bernhard Theodore Tobisch

Artwork copyright © 2025 by C&T Publishing, Inc.

Publisher: Amy Barrett-Daffin

Creative Director: Gailen Runge

Senior Editor: Roxane Cerda

Associate Editor: Karly Wallace

Proofreader: Second Glance Editorial

Indexer: Victoria Gregory - Chickadee Valley Editorial

Cover/Book Designer: April Mostek

Production Coordinator: Tim Manibusan

Illustrator: Tim Manibusan

Photography Coordinator: Rachel Ackley

Front cover photography by Shelley Tobisch and Bernie Tobisch

Photography by Shelley Tobisch and Bernie Tobisch, unless otherwise noted

Published by C&T Publishing, Inc., P.O. Box 1456, Lafayette, CA 94549

Attention Teachers: C&T Publishing, Inc., encourages the use of our books as texts for teaching. You can find lesson plans for many of our titles at ctpub.com or contact us at ctinfo@ctpub.com.

We take great care to ensure that the information included in our products is accurate and presented in good faith, but no warranty is provided, nor are results guaranteed. Having no control over the choices of materials or procedures used, neither the author nor C&T Publishing, Inc., shall have any liability to any person or entity with respect to any loss or damage caused directly or indirectly by the information contained in this book. For your convenience, we post an up-to-date listing of corrections on our website (ctpub.com). If a correction is not already noted, please contact our customer service department at ctinfo@ctpub.com or P.O. Box 1456, Lafayette, CA 94549.

Trademark (™) and registered trademark (®) names are used throughout this book. Rather than use the symbols with every occurrence of a trademark or registered trademark name, we are using the names only in the editorial fashion and to the benefit of the owner, with no intention of infringement.

Library of Congress Cataloging-in-Publication Data

Names: Tobisch, Shelley, 1963- author. | Tobisch, Bernie, 1953- author.

Title: Ultimate guide to sewing machine feet : choose, use, and troubleshoot your machine feet for success / Shelley Tobisch and Bernie Tobisch.

Description: Lafayette, CA : C&T Publishing, 2025. | Includes index. | Summary: "Explore the wide variety of sewing machine feet and learn how to use them effectively to get the most out of your sewing machine! Become an expert in using your sewing machine feet for various applications! Based on the popular class offered by Shelley Scott-Tobisch and Bernie Tobisch, the dynamic duo returns to teach you how to correctly select the right sewing foot for the job, use it for various applications, and troubleshoot common pitfalls. Whether you are a beginner or a seasoned crafter, this comprehensive guide offers everything you need to know to do more than you ever imagined with feet you probably already own! Discover the wide variety of sewing machine feet for quilting, sewing, and embellishment. Learn how to use which foot to make your life easier and your projects more polished with feet you probably already own. Gain problem-solving skills to troubleshoot common issues and enhance your skills in thread choice, tension, needle selection, and more"-- Provided by publisher.

Identifiers: LCCN 2024023327 | ISBN 9781644032213 (trade paperback) | ISBN 9781644032220 (ebook)

Subjects: LCSH: Machine sewing--Handbooks, manuals, etc. | Sewing machines--Equipment and supplies--Handbooks, manuals, etc. | BISAC: CRAFTS & HOBBIES / Quilts & Quilting | CRAFTS & HOBBIES / Patchwork
Classification: LCC TT713 .T623 2025 | DDC 646.2/044--dc23/eng/20240716

LC record available at https://lccn.loc.gov/2024023327

Printed in China

10 9 8 7 6 5 4 3 2 1

Dedication

*Dedicated to you,
the maker, and your
creative curiosity.*

Acknowledgments

Thank you to C&T Publishing for your tireless support and understanding while we navigated the circle of life during the writing of this book.

Thank you to Alex Anderson, FreeSpirit Fabrics, and Wonderfil Specialty Threads for generously donating stabilizer, fabric, and thread.

Thank you to our friend Patti, owner of Periwinkle Quilting & Beyond, for your endless support and for the use of your classroom and sewing machines.

Thank you to our friend Wendy, owner of Haus of Fabrics, for all your support and for the use of your classroom and sewing machines.

We are so grateful for each and every one of you.

Thank you!

Shelley and Bernie

Contents

ZIGZAG FOOT   39

OVERCAST FOOT   44

STRAIGHT-STITCH FOOT   45

ZIPPER FOOT   47

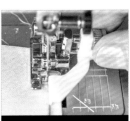

BLINDSTITCH FOOT   52

BUTTONHOLE FOOT   54

EDGESTITCH FOOT   61

EDGESTITCH FOOT   61

TOPSTITCHING FEET   64

JEANS FOOT   66

BUTTON SEW-ON FOOT 67

NON-STICK FEET 70

COUCHING/CORDING FOOT 71

FEET FOR PINTUCKING 76

GATHERING FOOT 81

PATCHWORK FOOT 85

EMBROIDERY AND APPLIQUÉ FEET 93

FREE-MOTION OR DARNING FOOT 100

WALKING FOOT 110

UPPER FEED MECHANISM 120

Introduction

Over the years we have taught many classes showing how to use the numerous specialty presser feet that are available from most sewing machine manufacturers. It is always gratifying to see the joy and excitement on sewists' faces when they see the great results that can be achieved by using the foot designed for the task.

Shelley demonstrates the creative uses of the foot and Bernie explains how and why the foot works and gives technical advice. Rather than just show how the foot works, we explain how needle and thread choices, tension settings, needle position, presser foot pressure and more, individually or in combination, can have an impact on the final result. We have carried this theme throughout the book. It is for this reason that we have used the words Ultimate Guide in the title. Our focus is more on the foot itself, what makes it work and some tips, rather than the entire technique associated with it. We also wanted to give pointers and help you avoid common pitfalls that we have run across in our classes. There is a lot of great information out there offering different techniques to make the best of these feet. To show them all would require many books.

Even writing this book in this way, we found that between the number of feet available and the variations across brands, combined with the amount of detail we wanted to give, it would be impossible to do justice to all feet in one volume. Don't be disappointed if you do not see a foot here that you are interested in. Instead, stay tuned.

We sincerely hope this book entices you to abandon the usual one or two presser foot choices and inspires you to open the door to the world of endless creativity that specialty feet offer.

The Feet We Used

We are not promoting any manufacturer; instead we wanted to show as many different feet as we could for each type. It would be impossible to show every brand's foot for each. But for each type of foot you should see a foot that you can recognize as being similar to the brand you are working with.

SAMPLES AND HOW-TO STITCHING

With the exception of the decorative embroidery, couching, denim, and stretch fabric examples, we used a size 70 HLX5 Organ needle and 50/2, long strand, 100% Egyptian cotton thread on FreeSpirit and Moda Fabrics 100% cotton fabric.

Terms and Descriptions Used in This Book

Throughout this book you will find the following sewing terms that you may or may not be familiar with.

APPLIQUÉ. A sewing technique in which fabric patches are layered onto a foundation fabric and then stitched in place by hand or machine. The raw edges can be turned under or covered with decorative stitching.

CHAIN/CHAINING/CHAIN PIECING. Chaining is transitioning from a seam on one piece of fabric to a seam on the next piece of fabric, without cutting the threads between pieces.

COUCHING. Couching is a technique used to attach decorative threads, cords, and other fibers to a foundation fabric. This can be accomplished using either a straight stitch, zigzag, or other decorative stitch found on your sewing machine.

DUAL FEED/IDT (INTEGRATED DUAL FEEDER TECHNOLOGY). An upper feed mechanism built into a sewing machine to help feed multiple layers of fabric.

FLAGGING. Flagging is when the fabric is moved up and down by the motion of the needle. This can cause skipped stitches, breaking threads, and what may appear as tension issues.

FOOT WOBBLE. For the purposes of this book, we define foot wobble as side to side movement of the presser foot.

HEADERS AND FOOTERS. A header is a small piece of scrap fabric used at the beginning of stitching. This small piece of fabric anchors top and bobbin threads. This ensures that by the time you get to the real seam all your stitches are locked in properly. A footer is a small piece of scrap fabric used to end stitching on. When you come to the end of your seam, before trimming the thread, sew onto a small piece of scrap fabric, ending with the needle down just off the edge of the fabric. Then trim all of the threads except those between the needle and the footer. The footer then becomes the header when you start stitching again.

HOPPER MECHANISM. The hopper mechanism is a feature in a sewing machine that slightly raises and lowers the presser foot while stitching.

HOVER. Hover is a feature on some computerized sewing machines that slightly raises the presser foot when the needle stops in the down position. This feature makes it easy to pivot fabric. It can be turned on or off.

NEST. Tangles of top and bobbin threads on the underside of your fabric. Usually created at the beginning of stitching.

PRESSER BAR. A presser bar is the bar coming out of the sewing machine that the shanks and presser feet attach to.

PRESSER FOOT PRESSURE. The amount of downward pressure placed on the fabric by the presser foot.

PUCKERING. Puckering is when a seam slightly gathers the fabric. This can happen when tension is too tight.

NEEDLE DEFLECTION. This occurs when a needle's path is altered by contact with dense fabric, a needle plate, or presser foot. This may damage all of these. It can be caused by a dull or imperfect needle point, an incorrect setting, wrong needle selection, or pushing and pulling of the fabric.

SCANT ¼" (6MM) SEAM. A scant ¼" (6mm) seam allowance is a wee bit narrower than a ¼" (6mm) seam.

SHANK. The shank is the portion of the foot that the sole is attached to.

SKIPPING STITCHES. A skipped stitch happens when the needle goes in and out of the fabric and a stitch is not formed. This will show as a longer stitch or no stitches at all.

SOLE. The sole is the part of the presser foot that comes in contact with the fabric.

TIE-OFF. Is a securing stitch at the beginning and or end of a seam.

TUNNELING. Tunneling describes when a zigzag or decorative stitch pulls fabric together from side to side.

METRIC CONVERSIONS
The metric measurements in this book follow standard conversion practices for sewing and soft crafts. The metric equivalents are often rounded off for ease of use. If you need more exact measurements, there are a number of amazing online converters.

Setting Up for Success

Choosing the right presser foot, presser foot pressure, tension setting, thread, needle, and needle plate (see Needle Plates, page 22) can make a big difference in the success of your project. A well maintained machine can make the difference between a good sewing day and a bad sewing day.

Presser Foot Pressure

How hard your presser foot pushes down on your fabric has a definite impact on your sewing. Too much pressure will stretch the top layer of fabric, making it longer than the bottom layer. If working with plush fabrics or batting, too much pressure will create a wave in front of your presser foot. As this wave reaches a cross seam it can create a fold. Too little pressure will create uneven stitch lengths and a feeling that the fabric is floating or wandering.

Top fabric longer than bottom fabric, too much pressure

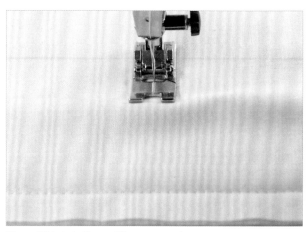

Wave of fabric in front of foot, too much pressure

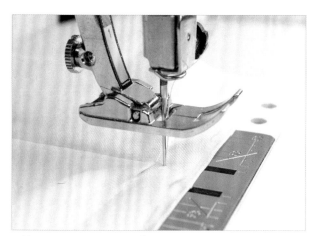

Fold over cross seam, too much pressure

Uneven stitch length, fabric floats and wanders, too little pressure

Some machines have a way to adjust the presser foot pressure. An important part of setting up your machine is understanding how your presser foot pressure adjustment works. If your machine has the ability to adjust presser foot pressure, it is a good practice to experiment and see the varied results. Learning how to use this setting can save you time and frustration down the road. Consult your user manual for the location and use of this adjustment on your sewing machine.

Bernie's book *You and Your Sewing Machine* (C&T Publishing) has a more in-depth exploration of this valuable feature.

TENSION

A properly calibrated sewing machine is a constant. We then throw variables at it — thread, fabric, and the task we are working on. We deal with these variables with needle choices and tension adjustment. Top tension has a range of adjustment from zero to nine. The default tension is usually near the middle of this range. Most machines with touch screens will have automatic defaults. Other machines will have a dial for adjustment.

Tension is a large topic and there is a complete and detailed discussion of it in *You and Your Sewing Machine* (C&T Publishing). The most important thing to remember is this: With the top tension adjustment you are controlling the position of the knot in the fabric. If you want to raise the knot, raise the number. If you want to lower the knot, lower the number. Knowing this will make top tension easier to understand.

In the how-to sections of this book there are times when we may give recommended tension settings. These settings are based on the premise that your machine is properly calibrated.

Balance Adjustment

Many sewing machines have an adjustment called balance. This provides a way to fine-tune feeding. Adjusting the balance changes the relationship between the forward and reverse parts of a stitch. For example, a decorative stitch where the machine sews part of the stitch in forward and part in reverse. Not every fabric feeds the same distance in each of these directions. This can result in stitches that look distorted and not at all like their illustrations on the machine. Adjusting the balance can match the stitch lengths and create a stitch that looks just right. Another place where this adjustment can play a role is with the buttonholes on some machines. If one row of satin stitching looks much denser than the other, adjusting the balance can even them out. Machines differ in how balance is dealt with, so it is best to consult with the user manual for your brand and model.

Light Maintenance

It is always good to know your machine is ready to perform at its best. Before you undertake a new project, it is worth taking the time to clean and oil your machine as shown in your user manual. In particular, check between the feed dogs with the needle plate off to ensure there is no linty "felt" build-up. This build-up can prevent the feed dogs from coming up all the way. One indication that this is happening is that fabric is not feeding properly, for example varying stitch length or inability to climb over seams.

PRACTICE SAFE CLEANING

The internet offers both good and bad information on maintaining your sewing machine. One bit of information that is both good and bad is using pipe cleaners and brushes with the small fuzzy heads.

These can be excellent tools for cleaning the bobbin area, provided that you do not dig around in areas you cannot see. We often see machines come into the shop with springs dislodged or missing due to enthusiastic cleaning.

Canned or compressed air is also not a good idea. Dirt and lint is blown back into the machine and gets lodged in places it should not be. A big fuzzy makeup brush is an excellent tool for cleaning the bobbin area of your sewing machine.

OILING AND WICKS

Some machines have wicks to distribute oil to the appropriate area. These wicks are often mistaken as lint and removed by diligent cleaners.

Wick in drop-in bobbin machine

Wicks in removable rotary hook

There are machines that specify an oil. Be sure you are using the right oil for your brand and model.

For detailed information on maintenance and troubleshooting of your sewing machine two excellent sources are *You and Your Sewing Machine* and *Sewing Machine Reference Tool*, both from C&T Publishing.

PLASTIC OR METAL BOBBIN?

Many drop-in bobbin machines have a black ring underneath the bobbin case. This ring is a magnet and is there to pull down the bobbin case to minimize rattling. These machines are designed to use plastic bobbins. Sometimes sewists will use metal bobbins as well. Metal bobbins are affected by the magnet and the bobbin tension will change. For best results, use the bobbins designed for your sewing machine.

Magnetic ring under bobbin case

Does Your Machine Need a Technician?

While there are many things you can do to keep your machine in good running order there are some times when your machine needs a visit to the technician. The issues listed below can make it difficult to use certain presser feet effectively. These adjustments need to be made by your technician.

Presser Foot Alignment

You might be surprised by how many sewing machines have misaligned presser feet. By this, we mean that the foot is not properly lined up with the markings on the needle plate. This can have an impact on seam allowances and how fabric feeds.

Presser foot not aligned

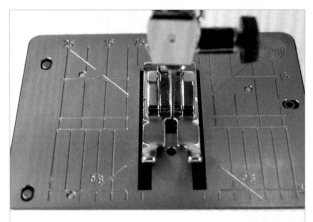
Presser foot properly aligned

Your technician needs to set presser foot alignment if you find yours is not right.

Needle Position

A very important setting is your sewing machine's needle position. In the center needle position setting, the needle must be in the dead center of the needle plate. If it is not, all the position settings will be off. This can be very important when using straight-stitch plates and straight-stitch or patchwork feet. If the needle is too far out of position it may actually make contact with the plate or foot. You may also find that you have inaccurate seam allowances.

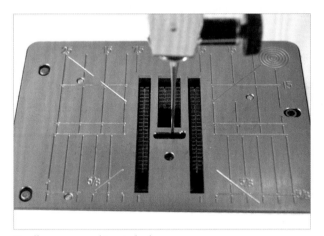
Needle not centered in stitch plate

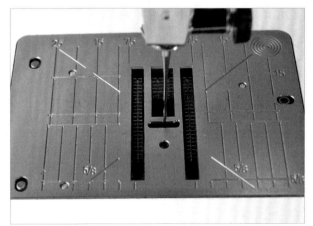
Needle properly centered in stitch plate

Your machine may have a setting for ¼″ (6mm) seam allowance. If your center needle position is off, this setting will also be off. Improper needle position needs to be adjusted by your technician.

Needles and Thread

Understanding the relationship between needles, thread, and fabric will contribute a great deal to the success of your project. We know that there are many types of threads and needles available on the market but for our purposes, we will be discussing the ones most relevant to the topic of the book.

NEEDLES

Needles are often overlooked as a vital element in the success of your creation. If your machine is in top working condition, but your results are not what you expected, the needle may well be the culprit. A mismatch in the size of needle and thread, or the style of needle and type of fabric can have a big impact. A dull or damaged needle point, a bent needle, or poor quality needle can create skipped stitches or even damage your fabric.

Information on Needle Packaging

A package of needles has information printed on it that can help you make good choices about which to use for certain threads and fabrics. This information and the order in which it is printed on the package will vary from manufacturer to manufacturer.

- Needle size, for example 80/12, tells you the needle size.

- Needle style, for example, 130N, tells you this is a topstitch needle (see Needle Style, page 13).

- In the case of twin needles, 80/2.5 tells you the size as well as the distance between needles.

- Needle system, for example 130/705H, tells you this needle fits a household sewing machine.

If you have a favorite brand of needle, it is a good idea to familiarize yourself with the way this information is presented.

Anatomy of a Needle

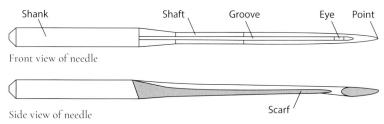

Front view of needle

Side view of needle

A simple way to understand a needle is to recognize that it has one relationship with thread and another with fabric.

Needle Size

There are two numbering systems for sewing machine needle size. An example is 100/16. The 100 means the needle is 1.0mm in diameter. Our research shows that the 16 is a Singer sizing system. Another example is 80/12. In this case the needle is 0.8mm in diameter. The smaller the numbers, the finer the needle.

Needle packages with sizes marked

The size of the needle relates directly to the thickness of thread you are working with. In the illustration of the needle, at left, you can see a long groove that runs from the top of the eye to the shoulder of the needle. For the proper formation of the stitch your thread must hide in this groove when the needle pushes down through the fabric. This ensures a minimal amount of contact between thread and fabric. If the needle is too fine for the thread, the result may show up as uneven tension or skipped stitches. If the needle is too large for the thread, the needle hole will be too big and your stitches may look slanted.

In the examples shown, the threads used are 100% cotton and the tension setting is exactly the same.

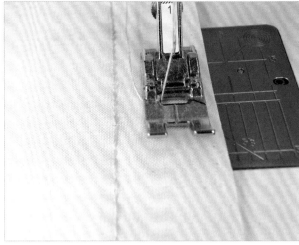

Needle too small for thread

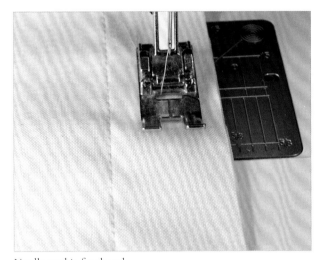

Needle too big for thread

Thread and needle matched

Needle Style

The style of needle often refers to the type of point, the shape of the scarf, and other design features. It is important to understand how these features relate to fabric and task. A knit requires a different point than a woven. A very stretchy knit may also require a different scarf shape in order to prevent skipped stitches.

COMMON NEEDLE STYLES

BALL POINT. This needle has a rounded point that makes it suitable for sewing on knits. The point slips through the fibers rather than cutting through them. This prevents damage to the fabric.

JEANS/DENIM. A jeans needle is designed to penetrate the dense fabric with minimal needle deflection. This prevents needle breakage and possible damage to the machine. Because a lot of denim now contains Lycra, jeans needles have changed from a sharp to a modified ball point.

MICROTEX/SHARPS. The fine tapered point makes this a good needle choice for microfibers and fine wovens such as Batiks. Many sewists use this needle for piecing and heirloom sewing.

STRETCH. Stretch needles have a ball point. The scarf and the eye are designed to help prevent skipped stitches on fabrics such as Lycra.

UNIVERSAL. These needles are the proverbial "Jack of all trades and master of none." The best results are always achieved by using the right needle, but in a pinch a universal needle may get you through.

LEATHER. Leather needles have a blade-like point that allows them to cut rather than punch through leather and leather-like fabric.

HLx5. We feel that these needles deserve a special mention. They are an industrial needle with a flat shank designed for household sewing machines and will outlast standard household needles. Their hard chrome, highly polished finish gives excellent stitch quality and adds to their longer life. HLx5s are more rigid and this makes them less prone to deflection. These needles are available in both sharp and ball point versions. The ball points are identified by the letters BP after the size. HLx5s are color-coded for easy size identification. Shelley uses them for most of her sewing.

NEEDLE CHART
This chart is a useful guide when selecting needle styles for common fabric choices.

Fabric	Ball Point	Jeans/ Denim	Microtex/ Sharps	Stretch	Universal	Leather	HLx5 Sharp	HLx5 Ball Point
Woven			X		X		X	
Denim (non–stretch)							X	
Stretch Denim		X						X
Knits	X			X	X			X
Super Stretchy Knits like Lycra				X				
Leather						X		
Vinyl							X	
Fleeces	X			X				X

There are some needles that we feel should be in this category due to their unique properties.

METALLIC NEEDLES. Metallic needles are specifically designed for use with metallic threads. They have a much larger eye and longer scarf than a regular needle. (See Anatomy of a Needle, page 12). The larger eye reduces friction, and the longer scarf lowers the chance of skipping stitches and shredding thread. Their eyes are either highly polished or specially coated to reduce friction.

⚠ CAUTION
If your brand of metallic needle has coating in the eye, we suggest you do not use your machine's automatic needle threader. The fine wire that extends through the eye to catch the thread may scratch the coating and create shredding issues.

TOPSTITCH NEEDLES. Topstitch needles feature a large eye to reduce friction and a deeper groove in the front of the needle to accommodate thicker threads (see Anatomy of a Needle, page 12). These needles are useful for metallic, monofilament, and the flat tinsel-like decorative threads such as Sliver and Hologram brand threads.

Some topstitch needles have a very sharp point and others a slightly rounded point. Check your chosen needle brand to see which applies. The sharp version would be best suited for tightly woven fabrics and the rounded for more loosely woven fabrics.

TWIN NEEDLES. Twin needles are two needles connected to one shank in order to create two rows of stitching at once. There are three important decisions to make when purchasing a twin needle. First, the distance between the needles; second, the size of the needles; and third, the style of the point. These needles can be used for straight or zigzag stitches.

Understanding Twin Needles

Your sewing machine must have zigzag capabilities in order to use twin needles, even if you are only using them to do straightstitching. There are some vintage sewing machines that, while they can do a zigzag stitch, will not be able to use twin needles. Check your manual.

Twin needles are available with the following distances between them: 1.6mm, 2.0mm, 2.5mm, 3.0mm, 4.0mm, 6.0mm and 8.0mm. The effect you are trying to achieve will determine the distance between the needles. Common tasks for straightstitching include hemming, topstitching (page 64), and pintucking (page 76). You can also create some beautiful effects by using twin needles with decorative stitches, in particular, if your machine has the ability to create 7mm–9mm wide stitches.

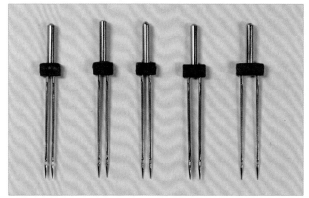
Twin needles

It is important to check your user manual to determine the widest twin needle that can be used in your sewing machine. Some machines will allow you to input the needle distance into the machine, which will automatically limit the stitch width so as not to break a needle.

If your machine does not have this ability, you must remember to subtract the distance between the needles from the maximum stitch width available on your machine. This number will be the actual maximum stitch width you can use without breaking a needle. For example, if your machine does 9mm wide stitches and you are using twin needles that are 3mm apart, the maximum stitch width you can use with twin needles is 6mm.

When selecting a twin needle you should also take into consideration your thread and fabric, just as with any other needle. Be sure to consider the thickness of your thread when selecting the size; see Needle Size (page 12). Twin needles are also available in the following styles: universal, ballpoint, stretch, denim, and metallic; see Needle Style (page 13). The style will largely be determined by the fabric being used and to some degree by specialty threads; see Thread (page 16).

THREAD

One of the most important lessons we have learned in our time in this industry is to recognize the attributes of thread and how they affect stitching.

Thread plays a much larger role in the outcome of a project than you might imagine. One thread may look much like another, but there are characteristics that will affect stitch quality and the overall appearance of everything from a straight stitch to a decorative stitch. Suppleness, smoothness, thickness, and fiber content of a thread all play a role in the final results.

Suppleness

Supple threads mold themselves to the fabric and can provide a more refined, softer look to the stitching. Because these threads are more easily pulled into the fabric, tensions are generally more consistent. Stiffer threads tend to lay on the surface of the fabric and may require tension adjustments to achieve the desired look.

The photos below show samples made using the same machine, needle, tension, and presser foot with two different 100% cotton threads. These threads are labeled as being the same weight and number of plies. The difference between these two threads is that one is more supple than the other.

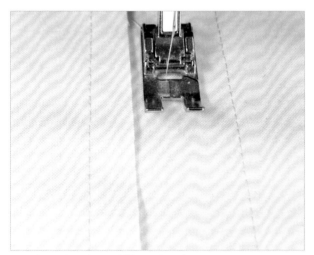

Straightstitch with two different threads—same settings, different result

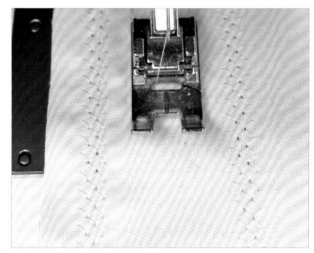

Honeycomb stitch with two different threads—same settings, different result

The preferred outcome is up to you. There are times you may desire a rustic result over a refined one or vice versa. Understanding the characteristics of your threads and how they affect the look of a stitch helps you make informed decisions. It is always a good idea to test samples until you are happy with the result.

Smooth Versus Lumpy

A smooth thread is one that is even in thickness. As this thread passes through the tension discs the pressure remains consistent. As a lumpy thread passes through the discs the tension varies. This may show up on your fabric as a tension issue. Not all smooth threads are supple.

Weight and Plies

For household sewing the most common numbering system for thread has two parts: weight and ply. Weight, the first number, refers to the thickness of the thread. There is a longer explanation, but the higher the number, the thinner the thread. For example, 100-weight thread is thin, while 12-weight is thick. Ply, the second number, refers to the number of strands twisted together to form that thread. On a spool labeled 50/2, 50 is the weight and 2 is the number of strands twisted together to form that thread.

If a spool of thread is labeled with only the weight, such as Cotton 50 or Ne 50, it will most often be a 2-ply thread. If you are uncertain and want to know how many plies are in a thread, untwist the thread until you can see the individual strands.

Threads that are labeled the same size may not be the same thickness.

In the photograph you can see 50-weight threads that have different characteristics.

Some of these threads are supple, some are smooth, some are lumpy, and some may have different fiber content. Even though they are labeled the same size they will show differently in your stitching. Taking a close look at your threads before you use them gives you more control over your outcome.

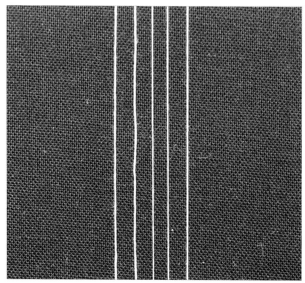

Selection of 50-weight threads

Fiber Content

The fiber content of your thread may have an impact on tension. At the factory your sewing machine's default tension setting was calibrated using a 50-weight cotton or polyester thread. Machines with auto tension have no way of knowing what thread you are working with.

Think of your machine as a constant and the thread as a variable. Once you introduce threads with different fiber contents and thicknesses than what was used at the factory, you may need to adjust the tension.

FIBER SLEUTH
Because labels fall off threads you may be uncertain about the fiber content. If so, do a burn test. Take the thread to the sink. Using a lighter, burn the end of the thread. If the thread burns, crumbles, and smells like paper it is most likely 100% cotton. If the thread melts and forms a hard bead on the end, it is most likely polyester. If the thread crumbles and smells like burning hair, it is most likely silk.

COTTON AND COTTON-LOOK POLYESTER

Although the look of the stitching is similar with these threads, you may find that when you use 100% polyester, the seams pucker slightly. If this occurs, slightly adjusting the upper tension may be helpful.

For best results, always be sure to match needle size to thread thickness.

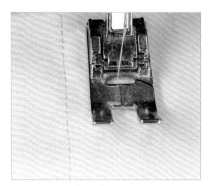

Seam sewn with quality 100% cotton

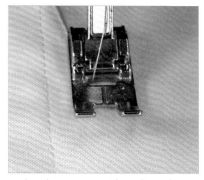

Puckered seam sewn with quality polyester at the same tension setting as the cotton

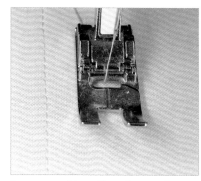

Seam sewn with quality polyester after adjusting top and bobbin tensions

In the monofilament category we are including threads such as invisible and flat, tinsel-like decorative threads. These threads may be made of polyester or nylon.

A common characteristic of these threads is that wherever they touch metal, such as thread guides, take-up lever, and tension discs, they grip. This greatly increases the tension on these threads. This will pull bobbin threads to the surface, pucker fabric, and increase thread breakage.

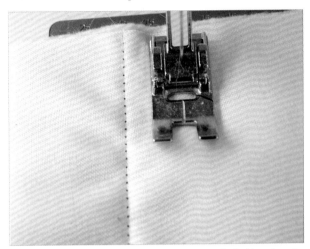

Monofilament before tension adjustment. Note the bobbin thread pulled to surface and puckered fabric

A good way to deal with this issue is to decrease the top tension to half of its normal default setting. This is a good starting point. Fine-tune from this setting.

Monofilament after lowering top tension

To further decrease thread breakage, using a metallic/metafil or topstitch needle can be helpful. The larger eye reduces friction on the thread.

INVISIBLE THREAD

There are times when using so-called invisible thread can be advantageous. There are two types available; nylon and polyester. Nylon will break down and become discolored and brittle sooner than polyester.

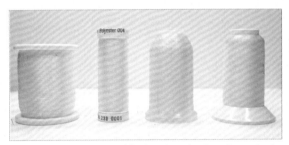

Nylon and polyester invisible thread—nylon has changed color

Metallic threads are often used for decorative work and can give beautiful results. They do, however, have characteristics that can make them challenging to work with. Not all decorative threads work well in a sewing machine. Some are very stiff and will leave loops on the underside of the fabric. No amount of tension adjustment will solve this. Due to the variety of metallic threads and their differing characteristics it is not possible to give accurate tension settings. It is always a good idea to make a test sample using the exact thread and fabric you will be using in your project. Start at the machine's default setting. If you are seeing loops on the underside of the fabric, increase the top tension. If you are seeing bobbin thread pulled to the surface, decrease the top tension. Make adjustments until you are happy with the results. Make notes on your samples as you are testing.

For these types of threads, using a metallic/metafil or topstitch needle can make a difference. The larger eye will help to lessen friction in the eye of the needle and reduce shredding.

If you have a beautiful metallic thread that will not work in your sewing machine, one solution is to couch it onto the fabric; see Couching/Cording Foot (page 71).

RAYON

Rayon threads are a great choice for decorative stitching, fabric embellishment, pintucking, and quilting. In fact, anywhere you would like to add a lustrous sheen to your stitching is a great place for these threads. You may need to use a slightly lower top tension setting. It is a good idea to do a test sample first. A topstitch needle in the appropriate size for the weight of thread is a good choice.

A good choice of bobbin thread when working with rayon thread is cotton or cotton-like polyester thread as these threads cling more to the rayon thread. A slippery thread in the bobbin like some very fine polyesters may tend to repel and tie-offs may come undone unless they are sealed with a plastic thread sealant such as Fray Check.

Contrast

Contrast, while not a property, can have a major impact on the appearance of your stitching.

Thread matching color of fabric

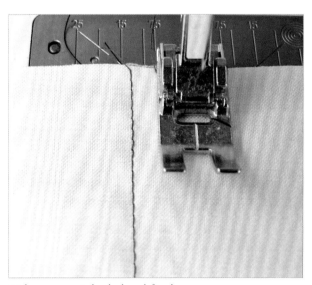

High-contrast stitches look undefined.

These samples were made using exactly the same needle and tension setting. In the high-contrast sample, it might appear like there is a tension problem, but there is not. This is how stitching looks when there is too much contrast between thread and fabric. There is no amount of tension adjustment that can fix this.

As you can see, as the stitching crosses different colors, the look changes even though the tension has not changed. The moral of the story is: Select your colors carefully and test them first.

Thread Delivery

When a thread twists it can create issues such as breaking threads and skipped stitches. When you are using normal-weight cottons and cotton-look polyesters it is usually not a problem. However, when switching to specialty threads, such as monofilaments and metallics, twisting thread can cause frustration.

When thread is delivered from a spool that is not turning, it will twist. Thread coming from a spool that turns does not. It does not matter whether the spool is cross-wound or parallel wound.

Dark thread on light and dark fabric—stitches look good on dark, bad on light.

Spool Pin Orientation

Most sewing machines have two spool pins. With some, the extra one will be in the accessories box. Often one of these will be horizontal and the other vertical. The spool pin you choose to use can also make a difference to your stitch quality.

HORIZONTAL SPOOL PIN

The horizontal spool pin does not allow your spool of thread to spin. This causes the thread to twist. This twisting can show up in your stitching here and there as a slanted stitch. With some threads, the twisting can be so bad that the thread creates a loop that can get caught in a guide and catch or break the thread. The benefit of this spool pin is that it is quiet because the spool does not spin. The advantages and disadvantages will need to be weighed by each sewist.

Prop showing how thread twists as it comes off horizontal spool pin

VERTICAL SPOOL PIN

The vertical spool pin allows the spool of thread to turn as it unwinds. This prevents the thread from twisting, delivering a more consistent stitch. The disadvantage is that it is noisier because the spool is turning.

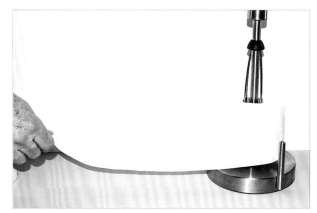
Prop showing how thread doesn't twist as it comes off vertical spool pin

ACCOMODATING LARGE SPOOLS

It is important to note that if you are using one of the larger spools of thread, such as the popular 1,300-meter variety, they are heavier, and you might have to turn down the top tension slightly until it is about half full. This is to compensate for the extra tension created by the weight of the thread itself. It is a good idea to have a spool pin felt under the thread to reduce friction.

REMOVE GLUE GUNK

The black stuff that you see on the vertical spool pin is glue from the label on the thread. This glue is very sticky and can stop the spool from turning freely. It is a good idea to clean it off with a tissue and some rubbing alcohol. This will help keep stitch quality consistent.

Vertical spool pin covered with glue

INDEPENDENT THREAD STAND

These stand-alone thread stands can be used for large cones of thread that don't fit onto the sewing machine. Even though they have a vertical spool pin, it is important to note that, because the thread goes first to a guide above the cone, the cone does not turn. This means that the thread will twist.

Prop showing thread coming off thread stand

PARALLEL-WOUND VERSUS CROSS-WOUND THREAD

Both types of thread work well. The reason I mention them is the belief that the cross-wound thread will work better on the horizontal spool pin. While it does work better than the parallel-wound spools, it still twists as it comes off. This is particularly true when the spool is closer to empty. Metallic threads and monofilaments will twist badly.

Parallel-wound thread

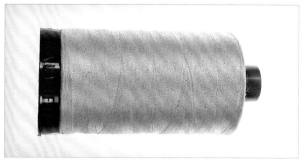

Cross-wound thread

If possible, it is wise to use the vertical spool pin to deliver the top thread. This will improve stitch quality due to less twist in the thread.

Needle Plates

The needle plate, sometimes also called a throat plate, is the metal piece that the feed dogs extend through to feed the fabric. There is an opening between the feed dogs that allows the needle to move in and out in order to create a stitch. The plate that comes with your machine has an opening that allows the maximum stitch width produced by your machine. The purpose of the needle plate is to provide support for the fabric as the needle enters it.

The right needle plate can play an important role in your success with a particular foot and technique. In each how-to section, we indicate if a needle plate, other than the one that came with your machine, will give you a better result.

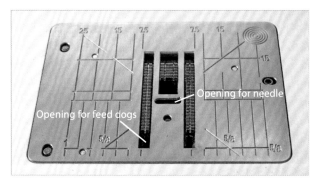

Needle plate

Needle Plate Anatomy

Most needle plates have markings for seam allowances, though some older ones do not. Some are marked in inches, some in millimeters, and some in both.

There are needle plates that have an opening to allow a narrow cord to be fed into pintucks. See Feet for Pintucking (page 76).

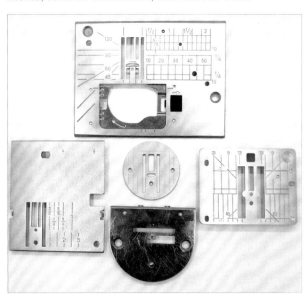

Needle plates with and without markings

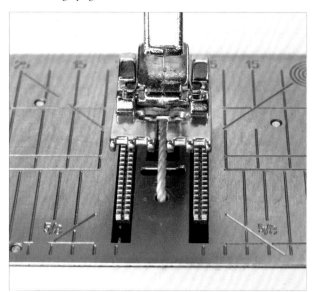

Opening for cord

Removing the Needle Plate

Some needle plates require a screwdriver for removal. Others have a spot to push down on or a place to lift. Still others need to be moved slightly forward and then lifted. There are some that need to be lifted in the front, with the feed dogs down, and then slid back to remove. Consult the user manual for your particular machine.

Needle Plate Styles

There are three basic styles of needle plates: zigzag, straight-stitch, and multi-purpose plates.

ZIGZAG NEEDLE PLATE

If your machine does zigzag, the plate that came with it will be a zigzag plate that matches the maximum width of your zigzag and decorative stitches.

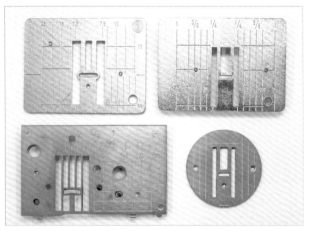

Zigzag needle plates with a variety of opening sizes

Many newer machines can create 9mm-wide zigzag and decorative stitches. This is a great feature and provides more creative options for the sewist. There are times, though, when this wide opening in the needle plate may create issues. Some of these machines have zigzag plates with smaller openings available. Using this plate can be advantageous when sewing narrower zigzag stitches, as it provides more support for the fabric and reduces the amount of fabric movement and tunneling. Machine appliqué, heirloom stitching, and overcasting are some examples where a plate with a narrower opening may give you better results.

⚠ CAUTION

Your machine may be able to utilize zigzag plates with different size openings. Make sure the stitch width you select is not wider than the opening in the zigzag plate you are using. Your machine may allow you to input the size of the plate, thus preventing needle breakage and plate damage.

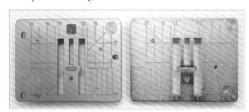

9mm and 5.5mm plates that fit the same machine

STRAIGHT-STITCH PLATE

This plate has only a small hole for the needle to fit through. The small hole gives the most support to fabric, which makes it ideal for straightstitching. This means that when the needle enters the fabric, there is minimal movement which gives better stitch quality. There is also less tendency for the needle to push the fabric into the plate at the beginning of a seam. This is important when sewing finer fabrics or when starting on a corner. When doing patchwork, the small hole prevents long, tapered triangle points from feeding into the needle opening.

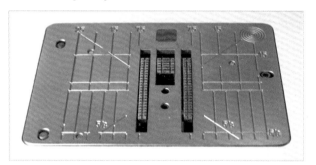

Straight-stitch plate

Needle pushing fabric into zigzag plate

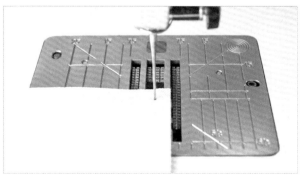

Fabric supported by straight-stitch plate

⚠ CAUTION

It is important to remember to only use a straight-stitch with a straight stitch plate. If you forget and select a stitch with any width, your needle may hit the plate and break. This could send a small piece of needle flying and may cause damage to the plate and/or the machine.

Some sewing machines have a switch that engages automatically when the straight-stitch plate is used. This switch limits the machine to straight stitch only. There are other machines that allow you to select a plate in the menu to prevent any accidents. The majority of machines, though, rely on you to remember that you are using a straight-stitch plate.

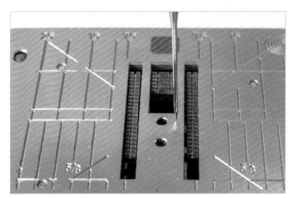
Needle about to hit a plate

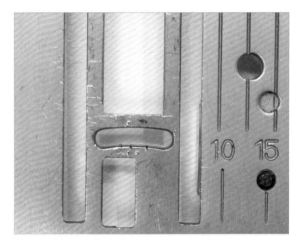
Damage from needle strikes

VISIBLE REMINDER
Use a sticky note to remind you that you are using a straight-stitch plate.

MULTI-PURPOSE NEEDLE PLATE

Your machine may have come with a multi-purpose needle plate. This means you can select a straight-stitch mode that engages a small sliding piece which converts the plate to a single hole, providing better support for your fabric when straightstitching.

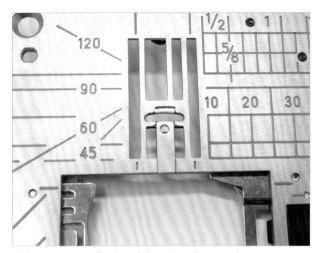

Multi-purpose needle plate sliding piece disengaged

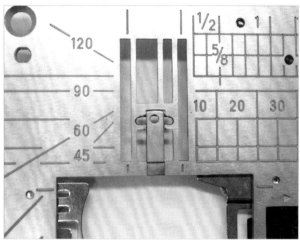

Multi-purpose needle plate sliding piece engaged

⚠ CAUTION

It is very important to know that if the needle hits the sliding piece it is possible to bend it. This can prevent it from engaging fully and may lead to needle deflection or breakage.

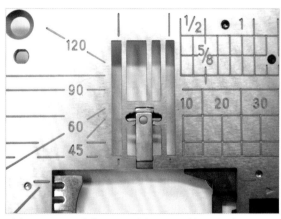

Sliding piece not fully engaged due to needle strike damage

Definition of a Presser Foot

A presser foot is the part of your sewing machine that holds the fabric down against the needle plate and the feed dogs to allow the fabric to feed. There are many varieties of presser feet. Each is designed to enhance creativity and make a specific task easier.

A presser foot consists of a sole and a shank, sometimes called an ankle.

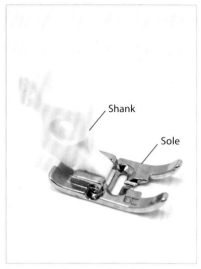

Presser foot showing sole and shank

Sole

The sole is the heart of the presser foot and its design can determine how easily a task is accomplished. Sewing machine manufacturers have engineered a wide variety of soles that allow the sewist to explore a world of endless creativity.

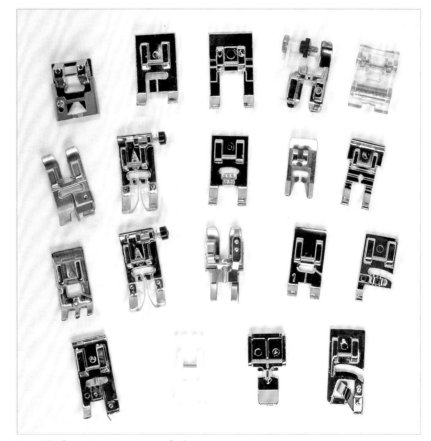

A world of creativity in a variety of soles

Shank

The sole fastens to the shank to complete the presser foot and allows it to be attached to the sewing machine's presser bar. Shanks can vary depending on the manufacturer. Some are defined as high shank, and some as low. Most are vertical, but some are slant. The style of shank is one of the factors that will determine which soles are compatible with your machine. Therefore, it is important to know which style is suitable before buying specialty soles. If uncertain, consult your machine's instruction manual to verify which style of shank will work with your sewing machine.

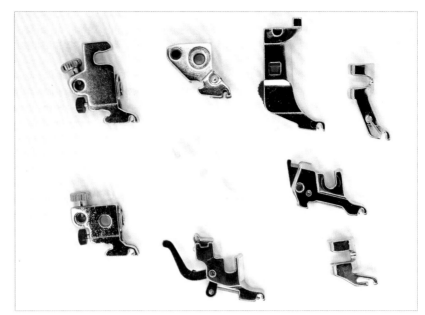

A variety of shanks

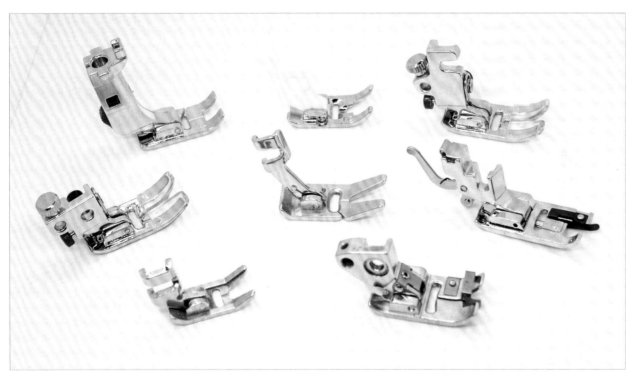

A selection of shanks with soles connected

The Purpose of the Presser Foot

A presser foot is lowered with a determined amount of pressure to hold a fabric, cord, button, binding, or a combination thereof, in place while the machine sews. For some tasks, it holds the fabric against the feed dogs for accurate feeding. For others, like a free-motion foot, it lifts and lowers to allow the user to move the fabric independently of the feed dogs.

Just as a sewing machine technician uses specially designed tools and gauges to keep your sewing machine running smoothly, the sewist uses specially designed presser feet. For example, you can sew a pintuck with your regular zigzag foot, but the result won't look nearly as polished as when using a pintuck foot.

Pintuck created with a regular zigzag foot

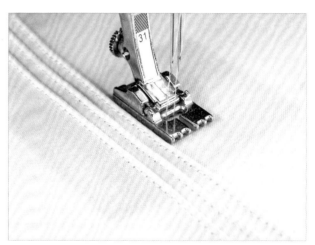

Pintuck created with a pintuck foot

Attaching Presser Feet

Presser foot styles can be subdivided into categories, defined by how they are attached to the sewing machine. Sewing machine manufacturers have engineered different ways to attach a presser foot. When buying specialty feet, knowing which feet fit your brand and model is important. In some cases, one brand's feet may fit another, but in many cases they will not. Having said that, it is possible that your machine may be able to be adapted to use other brands' feet. See Adapter Shanks (page 34) and Exchanging Snap-on Shanks for Use as Adapter (page 35).

FEET WITH PERMANENT SHANKS

This type of foot comes with the sole permanently attached to a shank. Depending on the manufacturer, the shank is then screwed or clamped to the machine's presser bar.

A benefit of this style of foot is that the sole may be more secure with less wobble. To expand the number of soles available, you may be able to use a separate shank that allows you to use presser foot soles that may not otherwise be available for your sewing machine; see Adapter Shanks (page 34).

Variety of presser feet with their own shank

Screw-on Feet

To attach these feet, you remove or loosen a screw in the presser bar. Some machines use a regular flat screw, and others a thumb screw.

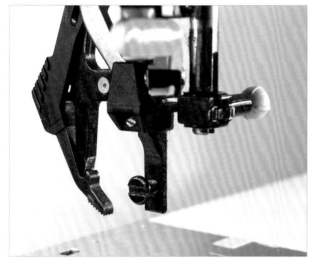

Presser bar with flat screw

Presser bar with thumb screw

HOLE ONLY IN SHANK

If there is a hole in the shank of the presser foot, the screw needs to be completely removed.

Screw-on feet with hole in shank

HORIZONTAL SLOT IN SHANK

Some screw-on feet have a horizontal slot in the shank. This allows the foot to slide onto the presser bar by simply loosening the screw.

Screw-on feet with horizontal slot in shank

Fastening foot with horizontal slot

A number of feet have a vertical slot in the shank. These feet slide up and under the loosened screw. While it is important to make sure all feet are fastened securely, this style of foot will slide off more easily if the screw is not properly tightened. Raising your presser bar to its highest level will make attaching these feet easier.

Screw-on feet with vertical slot

Fastening screw-on foot with vertical slot

Clamp-on Feet

This style of foot is attached by matching the opening in the top of the foot to the cone on the bottom of the presser bar. A lever is then engaged to hold the foot in place. This makes the foot very easy to change and very secure.

Clamp-on feet

Clamping mechanism on presser bar with lever disengaged

Clamp-on foot attached to machine, lever engaged

CODED CLAMP-ON FEET

In the clamp-on category of feet are ones that are classified by their manufacturers as coded. Coded feet have a lens that reflects an invisible beam back to the machine, which gives the machine information about the foot being used. It may identify the foot style, and then automatically govern needle position, stitch width parameters, and/or Dual Feed capability.

Coded clamp-on feet

SNAP-ON PRESSER FEET

Snap-on presser feet come in a number of styles. The common denominator is that the sole is separate from the shank. They differ in how the sole fastens to the shank and how it is released. Some machines have a low shank, some a high shank, and some a clamp-on shank. Refer to your user manual to determine which shank is right for your sewing machine.

Attaching and Removing Presser Foot Soles

Removing a sole from a shank that has a latching mechanism is done in a number of different ways, depending on the manufacturer.

A variety of snap-on feet

ATTACHING AND REMOVING SNAP-ON SOLES

The most common method to attach the sole to the shank is to lower the shank onto a bar built into the top of the sole. The bottom of the shank latches onto the bar with a latching mechanism and holds the sole firmly in place.

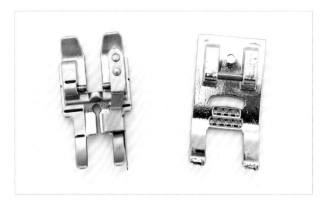
Presser foot sole with bar

Shanks with latching mechanism

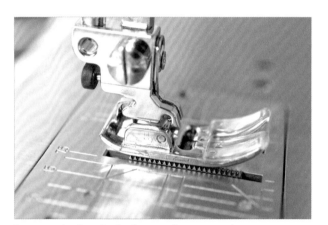
Lowering shank with a latching mechanism onto bar

Removing a sole from a shank that has a latching mechanism is done in a number of different ways, depending on the manufacturer. In all cases, the presser foot needs to be in its up position. Some have a lever, and some have a button. Both are pushed toward the presser bar. This action releases the presser foot sole. Another variation has neither a button nor a lever and the front of the sole is simply lifted to release it.

Shank with lever

Shank with button

Lifting up on front of sole to release

ATTACHING AND REMOVING PRESS-FIT SOLES

The press-fit version requires you to push down on the screw that holds the shank in place with enough pressure to fasten the foot.

Shanks with press-fit

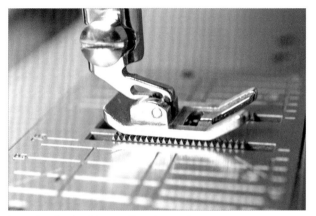

Lowering shank with press-fit style onto bar

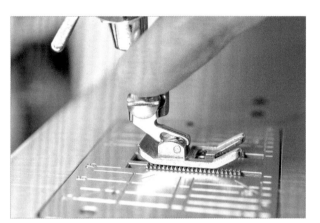

Applying downward pressure to engage fully

The press-fit type requires lifting up on the front of the sole to release it from the shank.

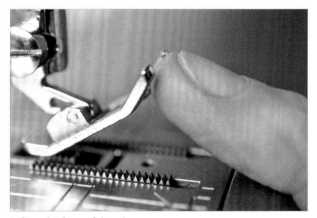

Lifting the front of the sole

SELECT THE RIGHT VERSION

Some press-fit soles come in low shank and slant shank versions. Refer to your manual to determine which is right for your sewing machine.

Another foot attachment variation uses a slide-on/slide-off method for attaching and removing the soles. The shank might be all plastic, or it might have a metal bar on the underside. This shank has a slot in the front. To attach the sole, push the bar straight into the slot.

To remove this type of sole, pull straight out.

Slide-on/slide-off shank

Attaching sole for slide-on/slide-off shank

Removing slide-on/slide-off sole

ADAPTER SHANKS

Your sewing machine brand may offer an adapter shank that allows you to use some presser foot soles that may not otherwise fit. Choosing the right shank allows you to use presser foot soles from other brands, which can greatly expand your machine's potential and your creativity.

Clamp-on Adapter Shanks

There are two styles of clamp-on adaptors. One snaps directly onto the presser foot sole. The other requires that the shank for the brand of sole being used be screwed on first, which may offer more versatility.

Clamp-on adapter shank that snaps directly onto sole

Clamp-on adapter that requires shank

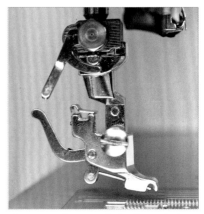

Clamp-on adapter with shank attached and ready for sole

Adapter Shank for Super-High Clamp-on Feet

We have included super high clamp-on shanks because they come with some very popular vintage sewing machines. This adapter shank converts the machine to be able to use low shank snap-on soles, after attaching a snap-on shank.

The adapter needs to be clamped to the machine and a snap-on shank screwed on.

Super-high adapter shank

Super-high adapter shank, with snap-on low shank attached

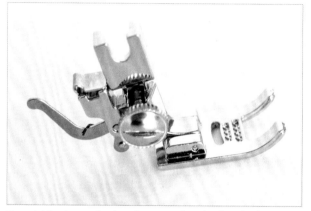

Super-high adapter shank with snap-on low shank and sole

Exchanging Snap-on Shanks for Use as Adapter

It is possible that you may want to use a specialty presser foot sole from another brand that fits onto your machine's shank. However, when you lower the needle, it strikes the foot. Exchanging the shank on your machine with the one designed for the presser foot sole may solve this problem. The shanks may look the same, but one positions the presser foot farther forward.

Another brand presser foot, too far forward, causes needle to hit foot.

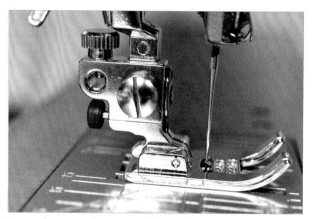

Presser foot properly positioned after exchanging shanks

There are many presser foot sets available on the market. Some include different shanks.

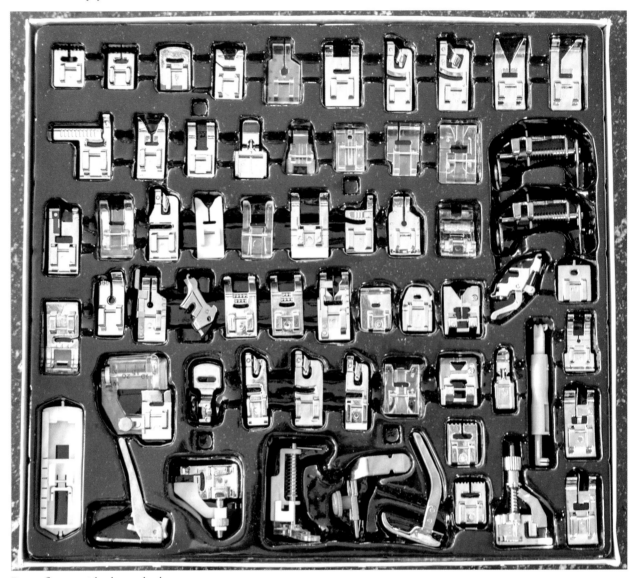

Presser foot set with adapter shanks

HANDY FEATURE
Some presser foot shanks have a white rectangle on the front facing the needle. This can make threading the needle much easier.

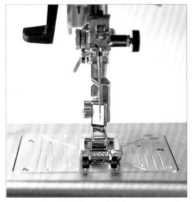

Presser foot shanks with white rectangle

Additional Sewing Machine Attachments

KNEE-LIFT/FREE-HAND SYSTEM

On many machines the presser foot can be lifted by a knee-operated lever. This can be a real time saver when stitching a project that requires a lot of pivoting of fabric such as appliqué, quilting, topstitching, edgestitching, and the like. When assembly line sewing, chain piecing for example, using the knee lift can be much more efficient than raising and lowering a presser foot by hand.

Most knee lifts can be slightly adjusted for the user's comfort. Some have a screw adjustment and others can be easily bent to the user's desired angle.

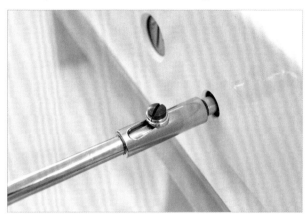

Adjustment screw

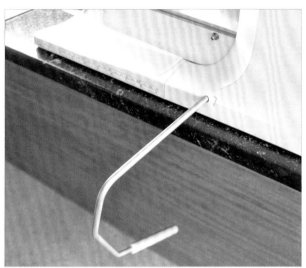

Machine with a knee lift

Some machines have the added feature of dropping the feed dogs when using the knee lift to raise the presser foot. This makes it easier to put thick fabrics under the presser foot, as the feed dogs are not in the way. The feed dogs reengage on the next stitch. Depending on your sewing machine, using the knee lift may also raise your presser foot higher.

LOUD CLICK MEANS A QUICK FIX

If your machine has a free-hand system that drops the feed dogs when lifting the foot, you will hear a click when the feed dogs come up on the next stitch. If this click sounds louder than normal, it may mean that the rubber O-ring that is used to cushion the sound has broken. This can be easily replaced by your dealer's technician.

SEAM GUIDES

Most sewing machine accessory kits include a seam guide. These guides can be helpful in maintaining a predetermined distance between seams or from the edge of a fabric. They may be used on the left or right side of the presser foot. Some guides attach to the presser foot shank. These can be held in place by a pressure plate or a set screw. Others are fastened to the bed of the sewing machine with a screw.

Guide held in place by a pressure plate

Guide held in place by set screw

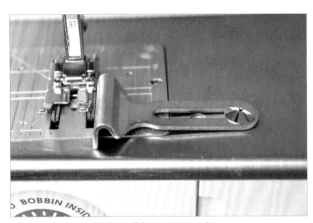

Guide fastened to the bed of the sewing machine

As an option, your machine brand may offer a left and right seam guide with measurements. For projects that require exact spacing in inches or millimeters, this guide can be helpful.

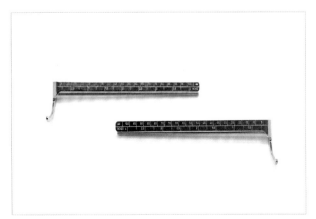

Left and right guides with measurements

Guide attached to foot

General Purpose Feet

Most new machines come with a small selection of general purpose feet. The number varies from brand to brand. In this section we highlight the most common.

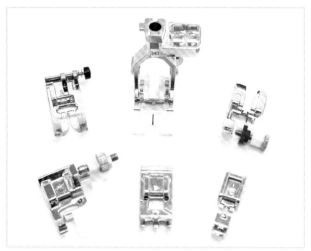

A selection of general purpose feet

Zigzag Foot

This foot is the one most often used and will most likely be on your machine when you take it out of the box. It is designed to work with many of the stitches on your sewing machine, from straight stitches, to zigzag, to decorative stitches. Some of these feet will be all metal, some will be all plastic, and some will be a combination of the two. The versions with plastic are designed for better visibility but may be more vulnerable to breakage from needle strikes.

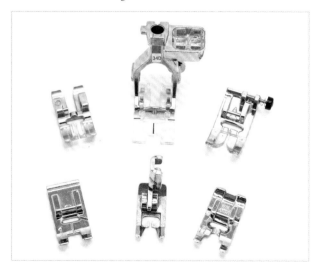

A variety of zigzag feet

This foot has some features that make it ideal for its intended purpose.

Needle Opening

The opening in this foot will accommodate the maximum stitch width of the machine. Different machines have different maximum stitch widths, from 4mm up to 9mm. To prevent damage, if this foot ever needs to be replaced, be certain you replace it with one that will accommodate the maximum width of your machine.

Needle opening does not match maximum zigzag width. Needle may strike foot

Markings

Many of these feet will have a mark or slot to indicate the center needle position. If this mark and center needle position do not line up, either the needle position or the presser foot orientation may need to be adjusted by a technician; see Does Your Machine Need a Technician? (page 10).

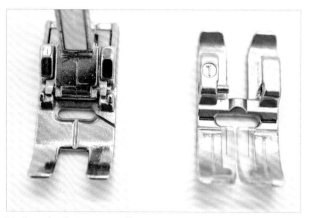

Mark or slot for center needle position

The Underside

The underside of this foot is engineered to hold the fabric down firmly and keep it from lifting as the needle is pulled up and out. This is called flagging.

Underside of a variety of zigzag feet

The Slope

On the underside of some zigzag feet, you will notice a slight slope from the needle opening toward the back of the foot. This slope allows the fabric to feed better when using stitches with some density, such as decorative stitches. Not all zigzag feet have this slope.

Zigzag feet with and without slope on the underside

The Thread Slot

Most zigzag feet have a slot, either in the front or the side of the foot. This allows you to pull the top thread into and under the foot. Threading the foot this way and holding onto the thread for the first stitch or two can prevent a nest on the underside of your work and keep the top thread from getting caught in your stitches. If your foot does not have a slot, it is wise to pull the top thread through the needle opening.

Thread into and under the presser foot.

TIP

If your foot does not have a slot for the thread, before attaching the foot to the machine, raise the foot high enough that the needle comes through the opening. Grab the thread tail and pull it down under the foot. Attach the foot and pull the thread into position so you can hold on to it when starting to stitch.

Needle through opening in foot

Pull thread through opening.

VARIATIONS OF THE ZIGZAG FOOT

There are specialty versions of the zigzag foot. These include non-stick, those with a leveling button, ones with the ability to work with a Dual Feed/IDT mechanism, and coded versions.

Non–Stick or Teflon Zigzag Foot

This foot has a special coating or is made entirely of a material that allows leather, vinyl, and other fabrics that tend to stick to the underside of a metal or plastic foot to feed smoothly and evenly.

The anatomy of the non-stick foot is similar to that of a regular zigzag foot.

Non-stick zigzag feet

Zigzag Foot with Leveling Button

Starting at a bulky seam or having to climb over one can be problematic. When the presser foot has reached its maximum angle, the fabric will stop feeding. This is when needle breakage can happen. Minimally, the stitch length will vary.

Some zigzag feet have a button on either the left or right side. It may be red or black. The button is used to level the foot when starting on a bulky fabric or when climbing a thick seam; see How to Sew a Bulky Seam Using a Leveling Button (page 42).

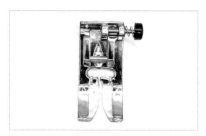

Zigzag foot with leveling button

ZIGZAG FOOT WITH LEVELING BUTTON ANATOMY

The button is connected to a spring-loaded pin. When the pin is pushed in, it locks the foot temporarily in a level position, allowing a bulky seam to pass more easily beneath the foot.

Close-up of leveling button showing pin

Dual Feed Version

Both regular and non-stick zigzag feet are available from some manufacturers to use with their version of a Dual Feed or IDT mechanism; see Upper Feed Mechanism (Dual Feed or IDT) (page 120).

DUAL FEED VERSION ANATOMY

This foot features an opening at the back to provide the top feeding mechanism of the machine access to the fabric.

Dual Feed/IDT version

Dual Feed/IDT engaged

Coded Version

BERNINA offers all these styles of zigzag feet in what they call a coded version. This coding provides the machine with information about which foot is being used. The coded zigzag foot informs the machine to allow the maximum 9mm width.

CODED VERSION ANATOMY

On the right side of this presser foot, you will find a lens. This lens reflects an invisible beam that comes from the machine back to the machine to provide information; see Coded Clam-On Feet (page 31) for more information.

Coded zigzag feet

HOW TO Use a Zigzag Foot

Using a zigzag foot is pretty straightforward. It will work for straightstitching and for varying zigzag widths up to the machine's maximum allowable width. In the following section, we describe how to use special features that are available with some zigzag feet.

HOW TO Sew a Bulky Seam Using a Leveling Button

1. Sew toward the bulky seam until the foot cannot angle up any more. At this point, stop with the needle down. **A**

2. Raise the presser foot and, pushing down in front, level it by pushing in the button and holding it in while lowering the foot. The button should stay in and the foot should stay level. **B–C**

3. Continue sewing. As the foot leaves the bulky seam, the button will release on its own. **D**

A. Presser foot at maximum angle, needle down

B. Level foot and push in button.

C. Foot down and level

D. Button is released and foot unlocked.

HOW TO ▸ Use a Non-Stick Zigzag Foot

This foot is an excellent choice when sewing with fabrics that tend to stick to the underside of a presser foot such as leather, vinyl, and more. Using a regular metal foot will create friction between the underside of the foot and the fabric, which will result in uneven stitch length, puckering, and difficult feeding.

The slippery substance that makes up or coats the non-stick foot glides smoothly over the difficult-to-sew fabric. This allows the feed dogs to do their job and evenly feed the material.

⚠ CAUTION
The underside of the non-stick foot can be easily damaged by the feed dogs. It is important to always make sure there is fabric between the underside of the foot and the feed dogs. Do not chain piece with this foot.

Uneven stitch length and puckering on vinyl

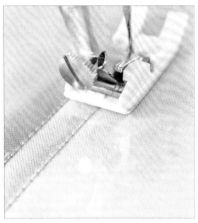

Even stitch length and no puckering

HOW TO ▸ Use a Dual Feed/IDT Zigzag Foot

There are a couple of things to remember when using these feet. It is important to engage the Dual Feed or IDT mechanism when this foot is on the machine. Sometimes fabric will push up inside the slot in the back of the foot if the mechanism is not in place.

The other thing to be aware of is that it is possible for the Dual Feed/IDT mechanism to catch on the fabric at the beginning of a seam. This may happen if you are starting to sew when not yet on the fabric. To avoid this, start on fabric and reverse back to the edge before continuing the seam.

Mechanism not engaged, leaving a gap for fabric to push up

Mechanism properly engaged

Fabric caught in Dual Feed/IDT

A coded zigzag foot will tell your machine whether it can use its maximum stitch width of 9mm. Once it is removed, the machine will limit zigzag width to 5.5mm. If the machine has a Dual Feed mechanism, it may also tell it that you are trying to use a non-compatible foot that has no slot for the Dual Feed mechanism.

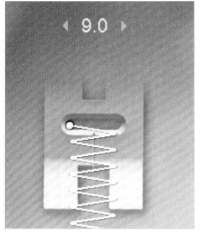

9mm stitch allowed with coded foot

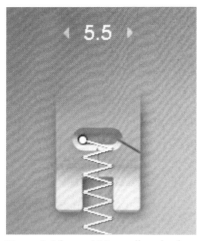

Non-coded foot and 5.5mm allowed only

Non-compatible foot message

Overcast Foot

Some brands include an overcast foot as standard with their machines. This foot makes it much easier to finish the edge of fabrics.

OVERCAST FOOT ANATOMY

The main feature of this foot is a guide that the machine sews over as the needle moves to the edge of the fabric. This guide can be a wire, a flat piece of metal, or in some cases look like a brush. For all of them the purpose is to hold the stitching out over the edge of the fabric in order to prevent a tunnel or pucker. Some of these feet have an adjustable guide and double as a blind hem foot.

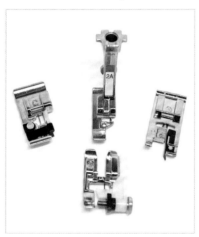

Overcast feet

Foot with wire guide and adjustment screw

Flat metal guide

Brush-like guide

Your machine may have some overcast stitches built in. Some of these are stitches that have forwardfeeding motion only. These work well for fabrics that are not stretchy. You may also have stretch versions of these stitches. These stitches move the fabric forward and backward and build stretch into the seam. All of them have a zigzag function, so using the zigzag plate is important.

1. Select the stitch that is appropriate for your fabric. Make sure the stitch width you select will allow the needle to clear the guide. **A**

2. If your foot has a guide for the fabric edge, set it to the distance you desire. **B**

3. Sew as desired. If you are using a stretch stitch, a foot with the wire or flat metal overcast guide may work better.

If you don't have any built-in overcast stitches a zigzag stitch will work nicely. **C-D**

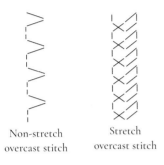

Non-stretch overcast stitch   Stretch overcast stitch

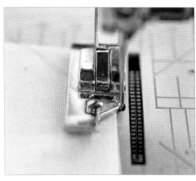

A. Needle clears the overcast guide.

B. Guide set to fabric edge

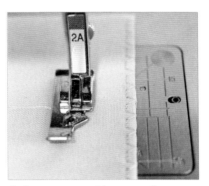

C. Overcast sewn with no tunneling

D. Overcast sewn with regular foot. Notice tunneling

Straight-Stitch Foot

The design of this foot makes it the ideal choice when straightstitching. Its profile allows it to feed well over heavy fabrics. This same design makes it good at sewing on fine fabrics that tend to pucker and flag.

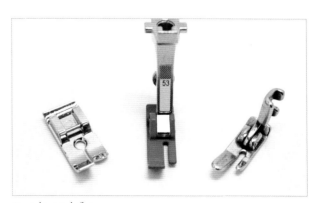

Straight-stitch feet

STRAIGHT-STITCH FOOT ANATOMY

Generally, a straight-stitch foot has one wide toe and one narrow toe. The edges of these toes can serve as distance guides for topstitch placement. The narrow underside of the foot creates less friction on the fabric and allows for smoother, more accurate sewing along curves. The space between the toes provides a clear view to the needle. Some manufacturers offer these feet in a non-stick version.

Straight-stitch foot showing narrow and wide toes

The Toes

The distance from the needle to the right edge of the foot is narrower than the distance to the left edge of the foot. This feature can be used to create a wider or narrower seam allowance.

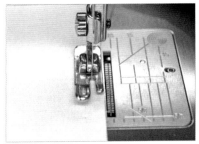

Using right edge as a narrower seam guide

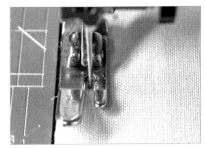

Using left edge as a wider seam guide

Straight-Stitch Foot Underside

The underside of this foot is flat, which provides a great deal of support for the fabric. There is also a narrow groove extending from the needle hole that will allow heavier threads to flow nicely under the foot.

Groove on underside of foot

NON-STICK VERSION

The non-stick version of this foot is designed for use with fabrics that tend to stick to the underside of a presser foot, like leather, vinyl, suede, and those with rubberized backing such as some rip-stop nylons. This foot may be white or green.

Non-stick version

⚠ CAUTION

Remember when using a non-stick foot to always have fabric underneath it. This prevents the feed dogs from wearing grooves into the foot.

COMPATIBILITY CHECK

If you have a zigzag machine, it is important that the straight-stitch foot covers at least one side of your feed dogs. This is usually the left side. Depending on the distance between your feed dogs, the right side of the foot may not touch the right-side feed dogs.

If your straight-stitch foot sits between the feed dogs, it will not feed properly.

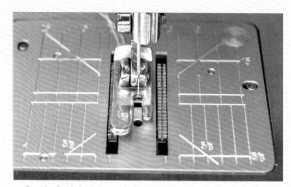

Left-side feed dog covered

HOW TO ▸ Use a Straight-Stitch Foot

If you have a zigzag machine and want to use a straight-stitch foot, the most important things to remember are to set the stitch width to zero and to set the needle position so that the needle is properly centered in the slot of the foot. If you forget, the needle may strike the foot and possibly damage both the foot and the machine.

When stitching with a straight-stitch foot on fine fabric, a straight-stitch needle plate can enhance stitch quality. It is particularly important when using this foot in conjunction with a straight-stitch needle plate that the foot alignment and the center needle position are calibrated properly on your sewing machine. See Does Your Machine Need a Technician? (page 10).

When using the non-stick version of this foot, remember that it can be damaged by the sewing machine's feed dogs. It is good practice to always have fabric under this foot and not to chain piece. This will increase the life of this useful foot.

Needle properly centered in the foot

Needle not centered and striking the foot

Zipper Foot

The zipper foot was created to help to make it easier to install a zipper. The foot is designed to sew a seam close to the edge of zipper teeth. It is also useful for inserting oversized piping cord; see How to Use a Zipper Foot for Piping (page 51).

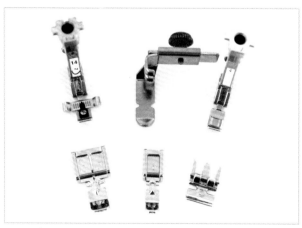

Zipper feet

ZIPPER FOOT ANATOMY

The bottom of the foot is flat to hold the layers of fabric and zipper tape securely. It may have a raised ridge on both sides to accommodate the zipper teeth. On both the left and right sides there is a cut-out, which accommodates the needle and allows the sewist to sew as close to the zipper teeth as desired.

Zipper foot with cut-out notches for needle

Flat underside and raised ridges on both sides

ZIPPER FOOT VARIATIONS

There are a number of different styles of this presser foot.

Stationary Zipper Foot

Some machines have a stationary foot where the sewist moves the needle to the left or right to fit into the notch.

With this style of foot, it is very important to remember to move the needle position to the side of the foot you are currently working with. If the needle is left in the center position, it will hit the foot, possibly causing damage to the foot and/or machine.

Stationary foot with needle in left position

Stationary foot with needle in right position

STATIONARY ZIPPER FOOT WITH ADJUSTABLE GUIDE

Some stationary zipper feet come with an adjustable guide for stitching along the edge of the folded fabric. The guide can be moved over the zipper coils to act as a guide.

Zipper foot with adjustable guide

Stationary Zipper Foot for Machines with Dual Feed/IDT

For some machines that have a Dual-Feed feature, a zipper foot with or without a guide is available. This foot has a cut-out at the back to accommodate the top feeding mechanism.

Zipper foot for Dual Feed/IDT

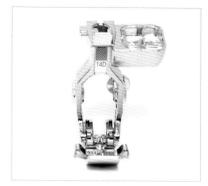

Zipper foot for Dual Feed, with adjustable guide

HOW TO ▶ Use a Stationary Zipper Foot

1. Fasten the foot to the sewing machine.

2. Move the needle position so that the needle is above the notch on the left or right side of the foot.

3. Select your desired stitch length. Selecting your needle to stop in the down position can be helpful if you need to stop and to slightly reposition your fabric or to pivot at the end of the first row of stitching.

4. Thread baste, pin, or tape the fabric onto the zipper tape, leaving the desired amount of space between the zipper teeth and the folded edge of the fabric (see General Information on Using Zipper Feet, page 51).

5. Lower the presser foot onto the fabric and zipper tape, and stitch. **A**

If your foot has a guide, it can be moved to ride over the coils of the zipper teeth for added accuracy. **B**

A. Position foot on fabric and stitch.

B. Guide riding over coils

Movable Zipper Foot

Some zipper feet move from side to side and the needle stays in the center needle position. The snap-on style has two positions, one for the left side and the other for the right side. These feet are also available for sewing machines with IDT.

Another type of movable foot fastens directly to the presser bar of the sewing machine and involves loosening a screw and sliding the foot from one side to the other.

MOVABLE SNAP-ON ZIPPER FOOT

This style of zipper foot has two positions, left and right.

For machines with IDT, the moveable style of zipper foot is available and will accommodate the upper feed mechanism.

Snap-on type with needle on left side

Snap-on type with needle on right side

Snap-on type zipper foot for machines with IDT

HOW TO ▶ Use a Movable Snap-on Zipper Foot

1. Fasten the foot to the sewing machine in the left or right position, whichever you prefer. The needle should be above the notch in the foot.

2. Select your desired stitch length.

3. Selecting your needle to stop in the down position can be helpful if you need to stop and slightly reposition your fabric or to pivot at the end of the first row of stitching.

4. Thread baste, pin, or tape the fabric onto the zipper tape, leaving the desired amount of space between the zipper teeth and the folded edge of the fabric (see General Information on Using Zipper Feet, page 51).

5. Lower the presser foot onto the fabric and zipper tape, and stitch.

Position foot on fabric and stitch.

SCREW-ON SLIDING ZIPPER FOOT

This style of foot has a screw on the back that is loosened in order to allow the foot to slide to the desired position.

Adjustment screw in back of foot

Sliding-type foot with needle on left side

Sliding-type foot with needle on right side

1. Fasten the foot to the sewing machine. Loosen the adjustment screw in the back and slide the foot into either the left or right position, whichever you prefer. The needle should be above the notch in the foot.

2. Select your desired stitch length.

3. Selecting your needle to stop in the down position can be helpful if you need to stop and slightly reposition your fabric or to pivot at the end of the first row of stitching.

4. Thread baste, pin, or tape the fabric onto the zipper tape, leaving the desired amount of space between the zipper teeth and the folded edge of the fabric (see General Information on Using Zipper Feet, below).

5. Lower the presser foot onto the fabric and zipper tape, and stitch.

⚠ CAUTION

Some of these zipper feet are available with a non-stick sole for working with fabrics that tend to stick to the underside of a presser foot, such as leather, vinyl, and more. To avoid damage to the underside of the foot, remember to always have fabric between the foot and the feed dogs.

General Information on Using Zipper Feet

This information pertains to all zipper-foot variations.

Tension with Zipper Feet

Some zipper tapes are stiffer than others. This may cause your stitching to look bad on the underside. The bobbin thread may not be pulled up into the fabric properly and result in a wavy effect. To solve this problem you may need to go up one needle size, increase your upper tension, or a combination of the two.

Needle

Use a needle style appropriate for the fabric you are working with in a size that complements the thread thickness; see the Needle Chart (page 14).

Double-Sided Tape

A great way to position the fabric onto the zipper is to use double-sided tape. It is important to use a tape that will not affect your stitching. A great choice that Shelley uses all the time is Dritz Wash-A-Way Wonder Tape.

Sewing Across Zipper Teeth

When using a zipper that you need to cut to size, it is sometimes possible to create a stop by sewing across the zipper teeth. This can be done on fine zippers with plastic or nylon teeth. Do not attempt this if the zipper has metal teeth.

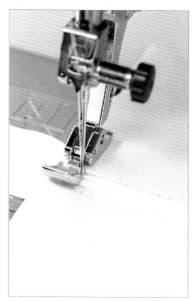

Sewing across zipper teeth

A zipper foot can be useful for inserting piping cord that is too thick for a piping foot. Fold the fabric around the cord and snug both up to the edge of the zipper foot. Stitch slowly, keeping the cord as close to the edge of the foot as possible.

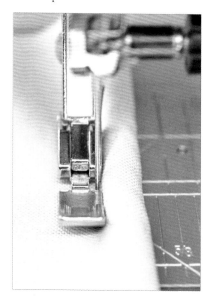

Stitch with cord as close to edge of foot as possible.

Blind Hem or Blindstitch Foot

The blind hem foot was designed to help create nearly invisible, professional-looking hems.

Blind hem feet

BLIND HEM FOOT ANATOMY

The most important feature of this foot is the guide. The guide makes it easy to keep the folded portion of the fabric positioned accurately.

BLIND HEM FOOT VARIATIONS

There are two main guide styles. One is stationary, which means that the stitch width will need to be adjusted for different thicknesses of fabric; see How to Use a Blind Hem Foot (page 53). The other style uses a movable guide where the fold itself is moved to account for the different thicknesses.

Stationary guide

Movable guide

In some versions of these feet, a guide runs through the needle opening. The zigzag portion of the stitch is formed over the top of the guide. As the stitch slides off the guide, another is being formed. The height of the guide creates a looser stitch, which means less puckering on finer fabrics.

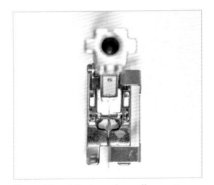

Foot with guide through needle opening

Foot with no guide through needle opening

Stitch formed over guide

HOW TO ▶ Use a Blind Hem Foot

The trickiest part of using this foot is getting the folds in the fabric right. For the best-looking finish:

1. First, make a fold to the inside of the garment. This will bury the raw edge. **A**

2. Next, pinch the fabric and bring it up and onto the first fold. Lay it onto the fold, leaving enough edge to sew on. **B-C**

3. Position the fabric under the foot with the second fold snug to the edge of the guide. **D**

4. Select the blind hem stitch. If your foot does not have an adjustable guide, move the needle position so that when the needle swings to the left, it barely catches the fold. The deeper it goes into the fold, the more visible the stitch will be on the outside of the garment. **E-F**

5. Stitch carefully! **G**

If your foot has a movable guide, adjust it so the fold is where the needle just catches the edge of it. **H**

It is a good idea to practice this technique before you try it out on a garment. It can save some stitch ripping. Play with the adjustments until you are happy with the finished result. **I-J**

When you have it right, the tiny stitch on the outside of the hem should be nearly invisible. **K**

Once mastered, you will find this foot very helpful!

A. First, fold to the inside.

B. Pinch and bring up to first fold.

C. Lay onto first fold, leaving enough edge to sew on.

D. Fabric positioned under foot with folded edge against guide

E. Blind hem stitch

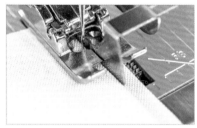
F. Needle positioned so it barely enters the fabric fold

G. Carefully stitched

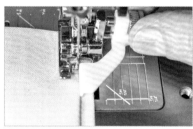
H. Guide adjusted so the needle just catches the fold

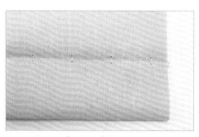
I. Needle too far into fold

J. Needle not far enough into fold and misses it

K. Just right!

Buttonhole Foot

As technology has changed, many advancements have been made in how a buttonhole is created. This means that buttonhole feet have changed as well. They range from feet that simply guide a row of satin stitching to feet that measure the buttonhole for you. The sheer number of different ways that manufacturers have offered buttonhole sewing, over all the different models and all the years, makes it nearly impossible to show how each of them work. In this chapter, we will describe the different styles of feet and what you should know about them. We'll explore how to fasten and set them up, as well as any special features. For details on how your specific model creates buttonholes, please refer to your user manual.

Different styles of buttonhole feet

MANUAL BUTTONHOLE FEET

This group of feet is designed for machines that have multi-step buttonholes. A multi-step buttonhole is one that is made by a machine that has you select each step and that does not measure the buttonhole length for you. The length is determined by marking the fabric or by a marker or stop on the foot itself. There are some machines that can use this foot for a stitch-counted, programmed buttonhole.

Manual buttonhole feet

As you can see from the photograph, the manual buttonhole foot is available in a variety of styles.

Example of machine with multi-step buttonhole

Stationary Buttonhole Foot

This style of foot allows you to sew buttonholes of any length, whereas a foot that has a sliding base is restricted in how far it will move. Some may enable you to add a cord into the stitching, which makes the stitching stand out and adds durability. The small size of this foot makes it possible to put buttonholes in tight spaces where the larger, movable foot may be too bulky.

Stationary buttonhole feet

What makes this foot work well are the grooves on the underside. These grooves are designed to guide the fabric straight. The raised line of satin stitches created by the machine sit in the grooves, which keeps the fabric moving in a straight line. Without these grooves, the fabric would veer and the two rows of stitching would not be parallel. This foot may be metal or plastic.

Grooves in underside of foot

Some of these feet may also have a center toe in the front or a post in the back. These are there to create corded buttonholes; see How to Make Corded Buttonholes (page 60).

Feet with center toe or post

Sliding Manual Buttonhole Foot

This style of foot has a large sliding base. This base provides stability and feeding accuracy to the fabric. Variations of these feet provide markings, indicators, or stops to help determine buttonhole length. The maximum size of the buttonhole is limited by the length of the foot. Many of these types of feet have the capability to make corded buttonholes.

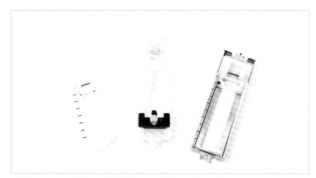

Sliding manual buttonhole feet with length markings

HOW TO ▶ Use a Multi-Step Buttonhole

For this buttonhole you can use either the stationary manual foot or the sliding manual foot.

1. Depending on your machine, select the stitch length and width suggested. Next, select the first step, often the first row of satin stitches. **A**

2. Select Step 2 and sew the bar tack. Don't sew too many stitches here, as they may pile up and impede the fabric feeding. **B**

3. Select Step 3 and do the second row of satin stitching. Be sure to stop where you originally started. **C**

4. Select Step 4 and complete the last bar tack. **D**

You may find that the stitch density is different on the two rows of satin stitching. If your machine has a balance adjustment, you can compensate for this difference; see Balance Adjustment (page 11).

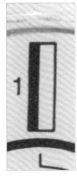

A. Step 1, first row of satin stitches

B. Step 2, bar tack

C. Step 3, second row of satin stitching

D. Last bar tack

PROGRAMMED BUTTONHOLES

Many modern machines have the capability to do programmed buttonholes. This is the ability to repeat the size until you have done all of your stitching. This is very convenient and gives excellent consistency. This category can be broken down into stitch-counted buttonholes and measured buttonholes.

Stitch-Counted Buttonhole Foot

A stitch-counted buttonhole counts the number of stitches you have made in the first row of satin stitching and then repeats this number in the second row.

HOW TO ▶ Use a Stitch-Counted Buttonhole Foot

Attach the foot. Select the buttonhole style. Touch the button that selects auto (see your user manual). Position your fabric and start to sew.

1. A stitch-counted buttonhole starts by sewing a row of satin stitching. It may begin or end with a bar tack. When you have reached the length you desire, stop. **A**

2. Touching the reverse button on your machine tells it to sew the second row beside the first. This tells the machine how many stitches to do for the next part of the buttonhole. It also programs the length so it is repeatable. It may first straightstitch back to the beginning before it starts to satin stitch in the same direction as the first row. Earlier versions stitch the first row forward and the second in reverse. **B**

If your machine is one that sews the second row of satin stitching in reverse, you may find that in some circumstances, the density changes and the stitching may overshoot or undershoot the bar tack. **C-D**

In this case, adjusting the balance can even out the stitching, so that the rows match properly; see Balance Adjustment (page 11).

A. First row of satin stitching with bar tack

B. Second row of satin stitching

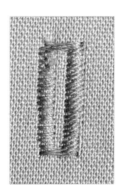

Completed Buttonhole

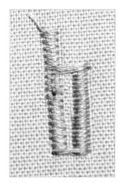

C. Overshooting bar tack

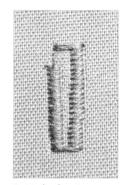

D. Undershooting bar tack

Measured Buttonhole Foot

Different brands of sewing machines have created different ways to create a measured buttonhole. Some use a coded lens to measure distance by how far the slide on the foot travels, some have you put the button in the foot as a measuring tool, and still others use a wheel that rolls on the fabric to measure distance. The main benefit of a measured buttonhole foot is that it creates more accurate buttonholes that are easily repeatable, giving the buttonholes on your finished project a more polished look.

Measured buttonhole feet

CODED LENS

This style of foot gives a very accurate, repeatable measured buttonhole and is very easy to use.

Coded lens foot

The coded lens on the right side of this foot has a fan-like device that revolves as the fabric moves and the base slides. This fan interrupts a beam that is sent from a lens directly above, on the machine itself. The number of times the beam is interrupted tells the machine the length of the buttonhole. This allows you to make accurate and repeatable buttonholes in the styles available on your machine.

In addition to the lens, this foot also has a soft rubber material on the underside. This helps move fabric evenly. On some styles of machines there is a sliding indicator on the left side of the foot to help program buttonhole length. Tabs are included on the front and the back to enable corded buttonholes.

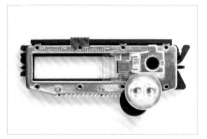

Lens and tabs for corded buttonholes

Lens on machine

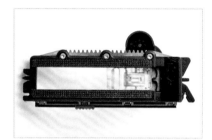

Soft rubber underside

HOW TO ▶ Use the Coded Buttonhole Foot

These feet do an excellent job of measuring and repeating your buttonhole. They have been used by the brand for decades and there have been many changes in the technology of the machines. This makes it difficult to list all the ways the different models make use of it. Please refer to your user manual to see how your model works with this style of foot.

SOME IMPORTANT THINGS TO KNOW

The lens on the foot and on the machine need to be kept lint-free for accurate measurement.

There is a sliding marker that can be used to help indicate where the buttonhole is in its progress. Just line it up with the length of the buttonhole. It is marked in millimeters.

Before starting to sew, be sure that the foot has slid all the way forward. It is on a spring-loaded slide, but sometimes it can inadvertently be pushed back.

Sliding marker

Keep sewing! This type of buttonhole is one step. The machine will stop when the buttonhole is finished. If you stop sewing before the last stitch is complete, the machine will want to finish the last buttonhole as you start your next buttonhole.

The foot that came with your machine is calibrated specifically to that machine. If the foot no longer measures properly, it may need recalibration. Recent versions of these sewing machines allow you to do the calibration yourself. In older versions you will need to take the machine and foot to your technician. If you have two machines that use this style, avoid mixing up the feet. Store each foot with its machine.

Some machines measure the button itself to give you the finished size.

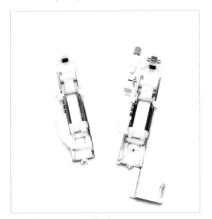

Feet that measure the button

This is a snap-on foot. On one end it has a piece that slides open to allow a button to be inserted. Inserting your button into the foot positions a piece that activates a switch. As the foot moves, the switch triggers all the phases of the buttonhole, including the long rows of satin stitching as well as the end bar tacks.

Buttonhole foot with button inserted

HOW TO ▸ Use the Button Inserted Foot

1. Slide open the portion that holds the button and insert the button. Clip the foot onto the shank. Be sure it is facing the right direction. Consult your owner's manual to be sure the orientation is correct. **A–B**

2. Pull down the switch actuator lever and position it per your machine's manual. **C**

3. Position your fabric and sew until the end of the buttonhole. Your machine may be programmed to stop automatically; check your user manual. **D**

A. Slide open piece that holds button.

B. Clip foot onto shank.

C. Position the switch actuator lever.

D. Position fabric and sew.

Another version of a measured buttonhole uses a wheel attached to the foot to measure the length of the buttonhole accurately.

Sensor foot with wheel

This foot consists of a presser foot with a wheel attached to the left side. At the wheel is a cord which plugs into the machine and electronically signals when the desired measurements have been reached. The teeth on the wheel ensure that it rolls properly on the fabric and precisely measures the buttonhole.

Buttonhole foot with wheel and cord

HOW TO ▸ Use a Measured Wheel Buttonhole Foot

1. Attach the foot by sliding it back into the shank. Plug the cord into the machine.

2. Select buttonhole style and length. See the user manual for your model. On some older machines, you may need to insert a cassette with buttonhole programs.

3. Position fabric and sew until machine stops.

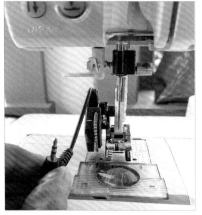
Attach foot.

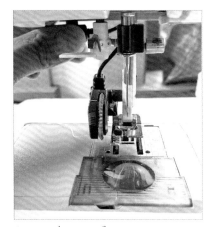
Connect the sensor foot.

Buttonhole Compensation Plate

There are times when making a buttonhole using one of the long sliding types of feet that the fabric may not feed properly. When the foot sits on a bulky seam, the feed dogs cannot make proper contact with the fabric. The buttonhole compensation plate was designed to help overcome this issue.

PLATE ANATOMY

This attachment consists of two metal plates that separate to hold the fabric on which you are making the buttonhole. It may have a rubberized bottom that allows the feed dogs to move everything evenly. The buttonhole foot fastens into this attachment or rides on top of it.

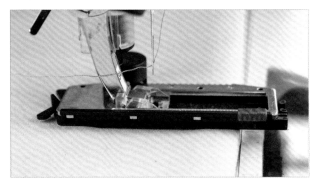
Long buttonhole foot sitting on bulky edge. Feed dogs will not feed fabric.

Rubberized bottom

HOW TO ▸ Use a Buttonhole Compensation Plate

1. Attach the foot to the plate. See your user manual for instructions for your model.

2. Attach the foot to the machine. Use the method for your model.

3. Position the fabric and sew the buttonhole.

Foot attached to plate

Foot and plate attached to machine

Position fabric and sew.

Many buttonhole feet have a way to include a cord in the stitching. Inserting a cord into the rows of satin stitching makes a buttonhole that is more prominent and durable.

The feet that are capable of this have a tab or clip-type device on the ends that holds a cord and positions it.

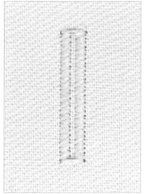

Buttonhole, not corded   Buttonhole with cording   Some feet with tabs for cord

1. Hook the cord into the tabs as shown. **A**

2. Set up the buttonhole in the usual way, as per your model. Sew the buttonhole. The cord will be inside the satin-stitched rows. Depending on the type of foot you use, you may have to hold the cord, lightly, at the back to keep it lined up. When finished, snip off the excess cord. **B-C**

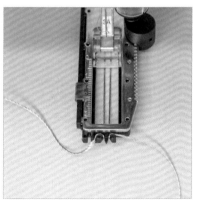

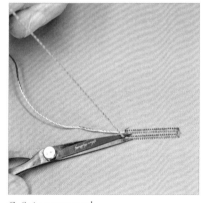

A. Cord hooked into tabs   **B.** Sewing buttonhole with cord   **C.** Snip excess cord.

STABILIZER AND INTERFACING

It is a good idea to stabilize the fabric when sewing a buttonhole. On finer fabrics in particular, the bar tacks on either end can tunnel the fabric. By adding a stabilizer, the stitching is kept flatter and the buttonhole looks much nicer.

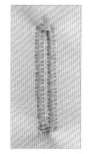

Bar tacks tunneling the fabric   Fabric stabilized and no tunneling

Feet for Construction

This category covers a number of feet that are designed for specific techniques. Using the appropriate foot can make achieving a professional result much easier.

Variety of feet for construction

Edgestitch Foot

Edgestitching is sewing a visible seam along a folded edge of fabric. This seam can be both decorative and functional, for example, stitching down a pocket or sewing along the edge of a collar. Beautiful and accurate edgestitching along a straight edge is best accomplished with a foot that has a guide.

EDGESTITCH FOOT ANATOMY

The true edgestitch foot is one that has a guide. Some have a guide that runs up to, but not through, the needle opening in the foot. The guide may be directly in the center of the opening or slightly off-set. Others have a guide on the right edge of the presser foot. On some feet, these guides are spring-loaded to allow for easier crossing of seams. Others allow very little up and down movement of the guide. Many edgestitch feet are available with a slot in the back to accommodate a Dual Feed/IDT mechanism if your machine has one; see Upper Feed Mechanism (Dual Feed or IDT) (page 120).

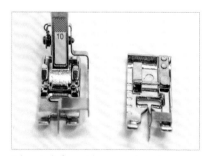

Edgestitch feet with centered, spring-loaded guide

Edgestitch foot with guide off-set to right of center needle position

Edgestitch foot with guide on right side

Edgestitch foot with Dual Feed/IDT slot

Select a stitch length. Place the folded edge of the fabric up against the guide. The type of edgestitch foot you are using will determine how you will adjust for the distance from the edge the seam is placed.

Place folded edge of fabric against the guide.

If the guide is stationary, you will move the needle position until you are happy with the seam placement.

Needle positioned into folded edge

If the foot has a movable guide, then you can adjust it until the seam is where you want it.

Guide in foot adjusted to position seam

It is a good idea to set your machine to stop with the needle down, if you have this feature. This will help keep the seam distance even when pivoting the fabric. If the machine does not have this setting, then place the needle into the fabric by turning the handwheel toward you when you reach a point where you want to pivot.

Looking at where the fabric meets the guide is more important than looking at where the needle is.

EDGESTITCH FOOT WITH DUAL FEED/IDT

If you are using an edgestitch foot designed for use with Dual Feed/IDT, remember to engage the upper feed mechanism. If you forget, you may experience feeding issues.

Bi-Level Topstitch Foot for Edgestitching

We include these feet here even though their manufacturers call them topstitch feet. Their design makes them great for edgestitching, but they may not be ideal for some topstitching.

Bi-level feet

BI-LEVEL TOPSTITCH FOOT ANATOMY

A bi-level foot has two levels on the underside to allow for even and accurate feeding when sewing on a folded edge — for example, sewing on a pocket. The higher level accommodates the folded, higher side of the fabric. The lower level acts as a guide that runs along the folded edge, maintaining a very accurate distance for perfect topstitching. Sometimes these feet come in a set of two, one for sewing along a left-facing fold and one for sewing along a right-facing fold.

Underside of bi-level feet

Edgestitching along a left-facing fold

Edgestitching along a right-facing fold

⚠ CAUTION

Bi-level topstitch feet that are ideal for edgestitching, should not be used for topstitching that is not also edgestitching. If the guide, the thicker portion of the foot, is not along the folded edge of a fabric, the pressure from the guide may slightly stretch the top of the fabric. This can create a wave of fabric in front of the presser foot, thus creating a fold as it crosses seams. In addition, the raised portion of a bi-level foot may allow the fabric to flag, causing skipped stitches and/or feeding problems. For how-to instructions, see How to Edgestitch (page 62).

ALTERNATIVE FEET FOR EDGESTITCHING

There are feet that were designed for other tasks that can be used for edgestitching. The common denominator is a guide.

Patchwork Foot with Guide for Edgestitching

Patchwork feet with a guide can be used to accurately edgestitch ¼″ (6mm) from the edge of a fold. Once you have stitched your first seam with the edgestitch foot, using the patchwork with a guide is an easy way to add a parallel row of stitching to a first row done with an edgestitch foot. For foot anatomy, see How to Use a Patchwork Foot with or Without a Guide (page 90).

PARALLEL ROWS OF EDGESTITCHING
When sewing two parallel rows of edgestitching, it is good practice to sew the seam closest to the edge first. This helps stabilize the top fabric for the second row of stitching and lessens the chances of puckering between the lines of stitching; see How to Edgestitch (page 62).

Patchwork foot with guide

Parallel rows of edgestitching

Blind Hem Foot for Edgestitching

Some blind hem feet have a guide that can also make them useful for edgestitching. Be aware that some guides run through the needle opening of the foot; therefore it is important that the needle is not positioned directly above the guide. See Blind Hem or Blindstitch Foot (page 52).

Blind hem foot for edgestitching

Topstitching Feet

The distinction between edgestitching and topstitching can be a bit blurry. In our view, an edgestitch can be a topstitch, but a topstitch does not have to be an edgestitch.

A topstitch is a visible straight stitch used to decorate any area on the surface of your fabric. The seam can be straight, curved, or meandering. Topstitching can be functional or decorative. Machine quilting, for example, could be considered topstitching. Using decorative threads can open the door to creativity and enhance the uniqueness of your project.

While you can topstitch with the zigzag foot that came with your machine, there are some feet designed to make specialty topstitching easy. Your best choice will depend on the weight of the fabric, the thickness of the thread, the type of fabric, and whether you are working with straight or curved edges.

Feet used for topstitching

CORDONNET FOOT

The cordonnet foot is a good choice when topstitching with heavier thread.

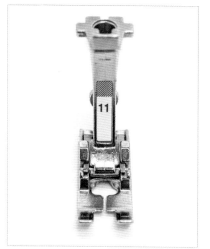

Cordonnet foot

Cordonnet Foot Anatomy

This foot has a specially designed underside. The cut-outs and groove can help when sewing with heavy threads.

Underside of cordonnet foot

THE JEANS FOOT

Some jeans feet have a groove on the underside. This allows heavy threads to feed properly under the foot. These feet can be an excellent choice for topstitching with heavy threads; see Jeans Foot (page 66).

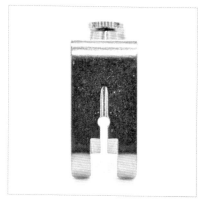

Jeans feet showing grooved underside of sole

NARROW FEET

A narrow foot creates less friction on the fabric, which makes it more nimble and an ideal choice when curves are involved. The straight-stitch foot and narrow patchwork foot can be helpful when topstitching curves.

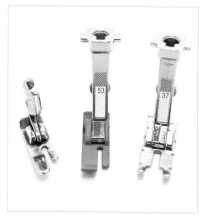

Narrow feet suitable for topstitching curves

Straight-Stitch Foot for Topstitching

A straight-stitch foot is an excellent choice for topstitching. Its narrow shape makes it ideal for accurate feeding, especially when sewing curves. When paired with a straight-stitch plate, it also helps improve stitch quality; see Straight-Stitch Foot (page 45).

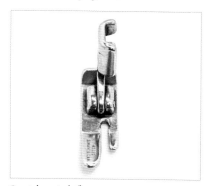

Straight-stitch foot

The Patchwork Foot

Most patchwork feet are well suited for topstitching, provided they do not have a guide. The narrower versions are an excellent choice when sewing curves. The wider ones do a great job when sewing straight lines. As a bonus, many patchwork feet have toes of different widths. The outer edge of the foot is ¼" (6mm) from the needle. The inner edge of the toe is ⅛" (3mm) from the needle. This gives the ability to accurately sew different distances from a previous row or an edge; see Patchwork Foot (page 85).

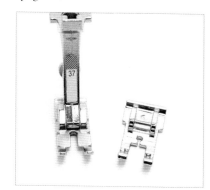

Patchwork feet without guide

Wave created by guide on patchwork foot

⚠ CAUTION

Feet with a guide, ideal for edgestitching, should not be used for topstitching that is not also edgestitching. If the guide is not along the folded edge of a fabric, the pressure exerted by the guide may slightly stretch the top of the fabric, which may create a wave of fabric in front of the presser foot, thus creating a fold as it crosses seams. The guide may also make it more difficult to sew a straight seam.

HOW TO ▶ Topstitch

Topstitching is very straightforward. You are using a straight stitch at a stitch length that shows off your thread. Remember to adjust the presser foot pressure if you are getting a wave of fabric in front of the foot.

Your machine may have a triple straight stitch, often identified as a straight stretch stitch. The forward and reverse motion produces three strands of thread, mimicking the look of one heavy strand. This may be a good option if your thick thread stash lacks the color you desire for the job.

Triple or stretch stitch

Triple stitch on fabric

If you desire to have topstitching that blends with your fabric, a good choice is 50–80 cotton thread. If you would like to have topstitching that is more decorative, a good choice is rayon, metallic, or thicker cotton.

TOPSTITCHING PLUSH FABRIC

If you are topstitching on fabric that is plush or has batting in between layers, a walking foot will be your best choice.

Jeans Foot

The jeans foot is a good choice when sewing through thicker, denser fabrics like denim.

JEANS FOOT ANATOMY

The underside of the foot has some design features that make it ideal for sewing heavier, denser fabrics. The more gradual curve of the toes and the very smooth underside allow seams to be climbed more easily. There is a narrow slot to accommodate heavier thread.

Jeans foot

When using the jeans foot, a straight-stitch needle plate is a good choice. Often, a heavier thread is called for, so remember to change to a needle size that is appropriate for the thread. The style of needle is also important; for example, use a sharp for cotton denim or a jeans needle for stretch denim. If the fabric is very dense and the thread is thicker, you may find that the bobbin thread is not being pulled up into the fabric or there are loops underneath. In this case, increase upper thread tension.

If the cross seams are thick, the fabric may stop feeding. If your machine offers the ability to adjust the presser foot pressure, now is the time to lower the pressure.

Too much pressure and seam is stuck at foot.

Ease pressure and foot climbs over seam.

This foot is also available in a coded version.

See also How to Sew a Bulky Seam Using a Leveling Button (page 42).

Button Sew-on Foot

Button sew-on feet offer a quick, easy, and accurate way to stitch on a button by machine.

BUTTON SEW-ON FOOT ANATOMY

This foot is specially designed to hold a button securely in place while being stitched. To aid in holding the button, some soles have a soft rubberized coating. Some have a center finger that creates a thread shank. On some feet, this finger can be engaged or retracted. Still others offer a height-adjustable finger. This allows you to vary the length of the shank. In order to fit through a buttonhole, a button on a fine silk blouse needs a shorter shank than a button on a thick wool jacket.

Variety of button sew-on feet

Button sew-on foot without finger

Button sew-on foot with height-adjustable finger

Sewing on a button by machine is easier than you may think. If your machine can do a zigzag stitch, you can sew on a button. Some machines even have a button sew-on function that is programed to stop and tie off after a certain number of stitches.

The size of the holes in your button will help determine the weight of thread, size of needle, and the number of stitches. If the thread is thick or too many stitches are taken, the hole in the button will fill up and the needle will get jammed.

Once the thickness of thread is determined, match the needle size to the thread. See Needle Size, page 12.

To keep the button from moving while the machine is stitching, you will need to drop the feed dogs.

If your machine did not come with this feature, it may have come with a feed cover plate. If it has neither of these things, then set the stitch length to 0.00mm. The button will still move up and down slightly while stitching, but it will not move front to back.

1. Position the button on the fabric and lower the foot onto the button.

2. Center the holes in the opening of the foot.

3. Select the zigzag stitch. **A**

4. Turn the handwheel of the sewing machine slowly toward you. Look to see where the needle is in relation to the holes in the button. You will need to adjust the stitch width to match the distance between the center of the holes. **B-D**

If the stitch width does not match the distance between the holes, the needle will strike the button, likely breaking both the needle and the button. E

5. Hold on to approximately 4″ (10cm) of top thread, and slowly stitch 5–8 stitches, depending on the size of the hole in the button and the thickness of the thread. **F**

6. Leave a 4″ (10cm) tail of top and bobbin thread. Pull both top threads to the back. Tie a secure knot with the tails.

A. Zigzag stitch

B. Position button under foot.

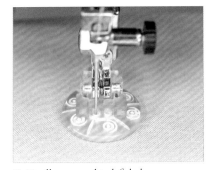

C. Needle centered in left hole

D. Needle centered in right hole

E. Needle striking button

F. Button stitched

UNIVERSAL STITCH

If you want your button sewn on more securely, the universal stitch is a good choice. This stitch will sew three straight stitches in each hole of the button between zigzags.

Follow the same directions as for zigzag stitching.

Universal stitch

BUTTON SEW-ON PROGRAM

If your machine has a button sew-on program, sewing on buttons is easy. The machine will sew a predetermined number of stitches, tie off, and finish. Some will even snip the threads for you. Consult your user manual for location of stitch and programming options. The set-up remains the same.

Button sew-on stitch

FOUR-HOLE BUTTONS

When sewing on a button with four holes, sew the first two holes and move the button for the next two.

Remaining two holes

HOW TO ▶ Use a Button Sew-on Foot with a Finger

This type of button sew-on foot is used the same way as in our previous descriptions. The difference is that the machine sews over the top of the finger to create a longer thread shank. The added length makes it easier to slip the button into the buttonhole.

The feet with height-adjustable fingers give more flexibility, enabling you to choose a shank length.

Stitching over adjustable finger

If your button sew-on foot does not have a finger and you would like to create a longer shank, position a pin or toothpick over the button between the holes.

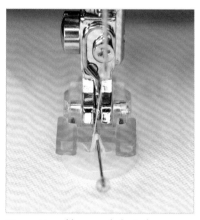

Pin positioned between holes in button

Non-Stick Feet

The many styles of these feet and their uses are covered in other chapters of this book, but we felt it important to give a thorough explanation of what sets them apart from their non-stick counterparts.

Non-stick feet are very useful for sewing on fabrics that want to stick and drag on the underside of a presser foot. These fabrics can include leather, vinyl, plastic, and the like.

Non-stick feet

NON–STICK FOOT ANATOMY

Some of these feet are made wholly from a very slick plastic and some have a unique coating that makes them non-stick. They come in a variety of styles, including zigzag (see Zigzag Foot, page 39), straight stitch (see Straight-Stitch Foot, page 45), zipper (see Zipper Foot, page 47), and embroidery and appliqué (see Embroidery and Appliqué Feet, page 93).

Leather, vinyl, plastic, and similar fabrics tend to stick and drag on the underside of a presser foot. This causes variations in stitch length and makes these fabrics hard to feed. Climbing seams becomes very difficult. The non-stick versions of presser feet allow these fabrics to feed smoothly and evenly.

Non-stick feet made from slick plastic

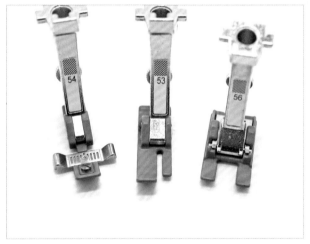

Coated non-stick feet

⚠ CAUTION

The coating on the underside of non-stick feet can be easily damaged by the machine's feed dogs. For this reason, always make sure there is fabric between the coated foot and the feed dogs.

Damage on the underside of non-stick foot

HOW TO ▶ Use a Non–Stick Foot

The non-stick feet will function the same as their regular counterparts. If you need to use one of these for a special fabric, look up the how-to section for that particular foot.

Feet for Embellishment

Embellishing fabric adds texture, interest, and excitement to any project. Embellishment can mean couching, beading, pintucking, decorative stitching, or simply straightstitching with decorative threads. It enhances your project and turns plain to pizzazz! Sewing machine manufacturers have created many specialized feet to help make embellishment easy and achievable. Understanding how your sewing machine, specialized feet, decorative threads, and cords work in harmony can lead to dazzling results and a lot of fun!

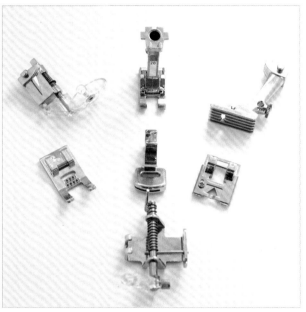

Feet for embellishment

Couching/Cording Foot

When couching/cording is done by machine, a decorative cord that is too thick to go through the needle is positioned onto the surface and stitched over with a zigzag, straight, or decorative stitch. Special feet are available for this technique. These feet are designed to guide the cord over the surface while stitching, thus making the process simple, accurate, and effective.

Couching/cording can be done with a foot that guides the cord or one that allows you to use free motion. These feet are available in single or multiple strand versions, as well as for thin to thick cords.

A variety of couching/cording feet

SINGLE FINE CORD FOOT

This foot was designed for single-strand, fine-cord couching. Notice the small hole in the front between the toes of the foot. Once the cord is threaded through this opening, it is guided into the proper position to allow the needle to zigzag directly over the top. Using a foot like this means less manual guiding and frustration. It makes beautiful results much easier to achieve.

Small hole for fine cords, yarns, and similar

Some couching/cording feet have a cut-out on the underside. This allows the thickness of the cord and stitching to glide effortlessly beneath the foot. The shape of this cut-out makes it much easier to steer the fabric as you create curves and shapes. A foot that does not have this cut-out is more likely to hinder feeding and make smooth curved stitching harder to achieve.

Cut-out on underside of foot

HOW TO ▸ Use a Single Fine Cord Foot

Attach the foot to your sewing machine.

POSITION THE CORD

How you position the couching cord before you thread it through the foot is important to prevent tangling.

Many machines have a knee-lift lever to lift the presser foot. Some cord spools can be positioned on this lever to allow them to turn freely. The cord goes directly from the lever to the opening in the presser foot. Be sure to keep an eye on this, so it doesn't get tangled or caught on its way to the foot.

Cord spool on knee-lift bar

If working with cord that is not on a spool or will not fit onto the knee-lift bar, find a spool of thread in your stash that will fit on the knee-lift bar. Wrap the cord around the spool and slide onto the knee-lift bar.

If you do not have a knee-lift bar, any spool of thread will work. Wrap your cord around the spool and place it on the floor or other surface where you can keep an eye on the cord as it feeds to the presser foot.

THREADING THE CORD INTO THE FOOT

Use a floss threader to make threading the small hole in the foot much easier. Once inserted into the opening, put the cord through the loop and gently pull through.

Using floss threader

SET STITCH WIDTH AND LENGTH

How you set width and length determines the final look of your couching.

Width

Select zigzag and set the width so the needle comes as close as possible to the cord on both sides without penetrating it. A helpful hint is to do a sample before you start on your project.

Length

Stitch length will be dependent in part on the thread you are using. A stitch length that is short will hide the cord. A stitch length that is too long will leave the cord loose. On your sample, try a variety of lengths until you find the most pleasing effect.

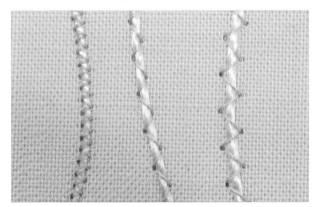

Different stitch width and length settings

In the above photo you can see examples of different stitch widths and lengths. Notice how they affect the outcome. On the left (short stitch length) the cord is completely covered by the stitching. In the center (longer stitch length) the cord is more visible with added texture. On the right, the stitch length is too long and the stitch is too wide. This detracts from the couching effect and makes the cord less secure.

SINGLE FINE CORD TENSION SETTINGS

Set the top tension so you can not see any bobbin thread at the sides of the zigzag.

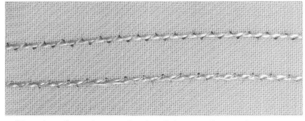

Bobbin thread not showing (top) and showing (bottom)

NEEDLE AND THREAD

Your needle selection will depend on the type of thread you are using. If you are using decorative threads such as metallics, rayons, and decorative monofilaments, a topstitch needle with its large eye is a good choice. For regular threads, use a needle in a size appropriate for the thread weight and a style to match the fabric; see the Needle Chart (page 14).

ALTERNATE FOOT CHOICE

Single cords can also be couched using multiple cord feet.

FEET FOR SINGLE THICKER CORDS, YARNS, AND NARROW RIBBONS

There are feet designed to guide thicker cords, yarns, cross-locked beads, and narrow ribbons. Manufacturers may assign these feet different names. Some are called couching feet, some braiding feet, and some piping feet. These feet will accurately guide one thick strand. A thicker strand can consist of multiple fine threads, cords, and yarns guided through the same opening or groove.

Piping feet are an excellent choice for guiding thicker cords and yarns. The piping foot will have a groove on the underside of the sole to help position the cord. The zigzag opening needs to be wide enough to allow for a stitch width that will exceed the thickness of the cord or yarn.

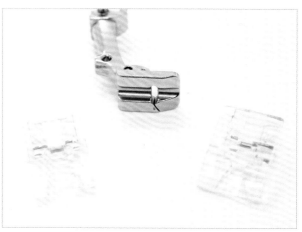

Single grooved piping feet

Thicker couching/cording feet

Some of these feet have a hole or guide on top. Their design allows them to guide cords, yarns, and narrow ribbons.

HOW TO ▸ Couch Single Thicker Cords, Yarns, and Narrow Ribbons

The basic instructions for using these feet are the same as those for single fine cords. Depending on the foot, thread the cord through the opening in the top or position it in the groove on the underside. Use a zigzag stitch at the length and width appropriate for the size of the cord. See How to Use a Single Fine Cord Foot (page 72).

Feet with hole or guide

MULTIPLE FINE CORD FOOT

To create more visual texture, manufacturers have produced feet that can guide multiple cords.

Some of these feet guide the cords via holes in the foot. Others use grooves covered with either a movable latch or a fixed guide.

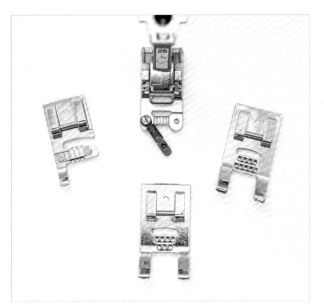

Feet with multiple guides

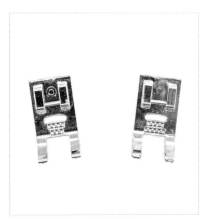

Feet with holes

Foot with slots and movable latch

Foot with slots and fixed guide

HOW TO Use a Multiple Fine Cord Foot

The main difference when using a multiple fine cord foot is that you will need to thread from one to the maximum number of cords that the foot will allow.

When threading the foot with holes for guides, use a floss threader; see Threading the Cord into the Foot (page 72).

When threading the foot with a movable latch, move the latch to the side, lay the cords along the grooves, and reposition the latch.

When threading the foot with slots and fixed guide, slide the cords under the guide to the desired slot.

STITCH CHOICES

There are a number of decorative stitches that work well when couching multiple cords. What we have found to be the best, and available on most machines, is the multi-stitch zigzag. You may find other stitches on your sewing machine that work well for you. Take time to play with different numbers of cords and decorative stitches.

Multi-stitch zigzag over multiple cords

Stitch Width

Select a stitch width that will cover the number of cords you are using. For example, with three cords your stitching will be narrower than with five cords.

Tension When Using Multiple Fine Cord Foot

Adjust top tension so you don't see any bobbin thread at the sides of stitching.

NEEDLE AND THREAD CHOICES

These are the same as for single fine cord foot; see Needle and Thread (page 73).

⚠ CAUTION

It is important to feed only cords that flow freely through the holes/slots. Attempting to use a thicker cord will result in inconsistent feeding, and a cord may get stuck in the guide. This stops the fabric from feeding and can create a thread jam in the needle plate, leading to the possibility of bent and broken needles and damaged fabric.

FREE-MOTION COUCHING FOOT

Adding visual texture to your project becomes even more interesting when using a free-motion couching foot. This foot enables you to move your fabric in any direction while stitching down a decorative cord or yarn.

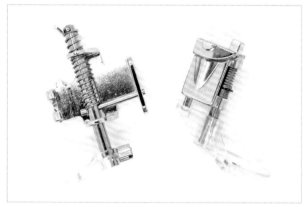

Free-motion couching feet

Free-Motion Couching Foot Anatomy

These feet work like other free-motion feet. Some have a large round sole, others a small round sole, and some have multiple soles to accommodate different weights of yarns.

Foot with large sole

Foot with multiple interchangeable soles

1. Thread the yarn to be couched into and under the foot, pulling it to the back of the foot. Using a floss threader can make this easier if the foot has a hole rather than a slot. If the foot has a slot, slide the thread into it. **A**

How your yarn is positioned will depend on your machine. Some brands have guides for this purpose for some models. The most important thing to remember is to keep the yarn slack so there is no pulling. This will help prevent needle breakage and jams.

2. If your machine has the ability to drop the feed dogs, do so. If not, set your stitch length to zero. If your feed dogs are down, it does not matter what length setting you use.

3. Depending on the brand of foot, select straight stitch or a narrow zigzag (no wider than 1.5mm). Check the specific instructions for your machine and foot.

4. Position the fabric and lower the foot.

5. Slowly start stitching. Remember, your feed dogs are down and you are in control of the fabric and stitch length. Move the fabric in any direction that pleases you. You are limited only by your imagination. **B**

A. Threading the foot with a floss threader

B. Moving the fabric and stitching down the yarn

CHOOSING YOUR YARN

If your yarn or cord choice is too thin, the needle may miss it when there are directional changes. If your yarn is too thick, it may stick or jam in the opening, making it difficult to move your fabric smoothly.

Your foot may come with special guides for yarn. Check your machine's manual for proper installation of these guides. Manufacturers' websites are very helpful.

Feet for Pintucking

Pintucking is a decorative technique that can turn an ordinary piece of fabric into something extraordinary. One description of a pintuck is a narrow decorative fold. However, pintucks can also surround a cord, making the tuck round and well defined. The number of pintuck feet available enable you to work with a variety of fabrics, from lightweight to more substantial. Pintuck feet are used in conjunction with twin needles; see Understanding Twin Needles (page 15).

A selection of pintuck feet

PINTUCKING FOOT ANATOMY

This foot is used in conjunction with a twin needle. A series of grooves run the length of the underside. The size and number of grooves determine the size of the pintuck as well as the distance between the twin needles used. The wider the grooves, the wider the needles will be apart. The grooves can be used to position previous tucks and create precise, parallel rows.

TWIN NEEDLES

Twin needles are available in many sizes; see Understanding Twin Needles (page 15). To select the right size twin needle for the pintuck foot you are using, place the needle in the grooves on the underside of the foot. If the needles lay in the grooves as pictured, then that is the correct needle to use with that particular pintuck foot.

Underside of pintuck foot with paired twin needle

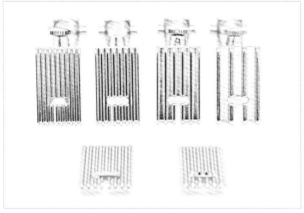

Underside of pintuck feet showing grooves

PINTUCK FOOT WITH THREE GROOVES

The grooves in this foot are wide. This allows it to accommodate thicker fabrics such as denim and linen.

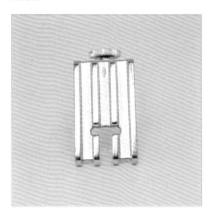

Three-groove pintuck foot

PINTUCK FOOT WITH FIVE GROOVES

This foot is one of the most commonly used pintuck feet. With it you can pintuck on a variety of medium-weight fabrics.

Five-groove pintuck foot

PINTUCK FOOT WITH SEVEN GROOVES

The seven-groove pintuck foot is the other most commonly used pintuck foot. The size of the grooves makes it ideal for lightweight fabrics.

Seven-groove pintuck foot

PINTUCK FOOT WITH NINE GROOVES

The nine-groove pintuck foot is perfect for heirloom work. Its narrow grooves work well with fine fabrics.

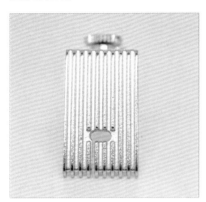

Nine-groove pintuck foot

CORDED PINTUCK GUIDE

Some manufacturers offer a guide for the cords that can be inserted into a pintuck. This makes cord positioning much easier.

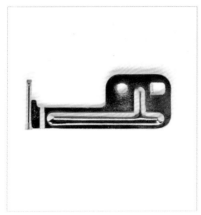

Pintuck cord guides

TIP
The needle plate on your sewing machine may have a hole in front of the needle opening. If you have a front-loading bobbin case on your sewing machine, you may be able to feed a cord up to and through this opening and under the pintuck foot. Leave the bobbin door open when sewing. If you have a low bobbin indicator, you may need to turn it off. Remember to turn it back on after you are finished creating your pintucks.

HOW TO ▶ Use a Pintuck Foot

These instructions are for a corded pintuck. For a regular pintuck, leave out the cord references. We are showing a five-groove pintuck foot and the appropriate twin needle with a distance of 2.5mm. The instructions for other pintuck feet will be mostly the same, the difference being the size of the cord and the distance between needles.

SET UP THE MACHINE

Positioning the Cord

A corded pintuck requires that a cord be positioned under or ahead of the foot and be guided into the center groove. Depending on your machine, this is achieved in different ways.

Through the Needle Plate

Open the bobbin door. Remove the needle plate. Thread the cord up through the bobbin area and into and through the hole in the needle plate. Place the plate back on your machine. Leave the bobbin door open.

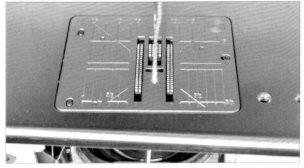

Thread cord through hole in needle plate.

Through a Guide

Your machine brand may offer an accessory guide that is positioned in front of the presser foot. Position the guide onto your needle plate. Feed the cord through the guide.

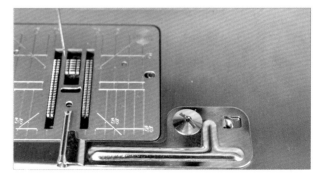

Guide attached to plate

If a guide is not available for your machine, a narrow plastic tube or straw, cut to length and taped in front of the foot, will be helpful.

You may be able to feed the cord from your knee lift; see Position the Cord (page 72). It is important to make sure that it can flow freely. Special care is necessary, as the cord will be hidden under the fabric. Check on it frequently.

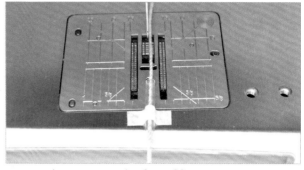

Narrow tube or straw taped in front of foot

Threading

Pintucking requires two top threads. Most machines have two spool pins. If your second spool pin is not permanently mounted on your machine, it should be in your accessory kit. Check your user manual. Place one spool onto the spool pin farthest to the right. Begin threading as usual. When you reach the tension discs, you may find your machine has a metal spacer in between them. This creates a separate tension for each thread. Place the thread on the right side of the spacer. Continue threading as usual and thread the right needle. Take thread to the back of the machine, under the presser foot.

Thread on right side of the spacer

When threading the second spool, place the thread on the left side of the tension disc spacer. Continue threading as usual. Thread the left needle. Take the thread toward the

back of the machine, under the presser foot.

Thread on left side of the spacer

NO SPACER?

If your machine does not have the spacer in the tension discs, thread as usual.

Have your threads come off your spool pins in the direction that creates the least amount of interference between them.

THREADING TIPS

If you only have one spool of thread, wind some thread onto a bobbin to use as a second spool.

If you only have one spool pin you can buy a thread stand that sits behind your sewing machine.

⚠ CAUTION

In our classes, we often find that when people are threading their machine for twin needle stitching, they will forget to put one of the two threads into the take-up lever. This is the lever that moves up and down on the front of the machine as you sew. We are not sure why this happens but we know that it will cause a big tangled mess at the beginning of your stitching and you will have to start threading all over again. Make sure both threads get into the take-up lever.

Take-up lever with two threads

1. Set the stitch length between 2.5mm and 3mm.

2. Make sure the cord is feeding toward the back of the foot. Make sure the threads are pulled to the back of the foot.

3. Bring the bobbin thread up through the needle plate and pull to the back. To pull up the bobbin thread, hold on to the top threads behind the presser foot and push the needle up/down button twice. This will pull up the bobbin thread and position the needles to start forming a stitch without tangling at the beginning of the seam. If you have a machine without the needle up/down feature, then turn the handwheel toward you, one complete turn, stopping with the take-up lever right at the top.

4. Holding all the threads and the cord, begin stitching slowly. If you have a tangle, review your set-up to see if you missed anything. **A**

5. When you reach the end of your stitching, raise the presser foot and pull the threads and the cord to the back. Cut them, leaving enough length that you can start again. You may decide to just leave a loop without cutting. Lower the foot and start the next tuck. **B–C**

A. Hold threads and cord and start sewing.

B. Cut threads and cord, leaving length.

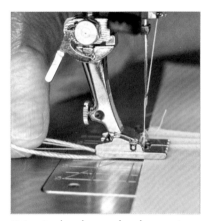

C. Leaving long loop, rather than cutting

PREVENTING A TANGLED MESS

If you do not have the feature that allows you to specify that the needle stops in the up position, remember to turn the handwheel toward you until the take-up lever is at its highest position before pulling out the fabric. If you don't, there is a good chance everything will tangle when you begin your next row of stitching.

Using the Grooves as a Guide

The grooves under the pintuck foot can be used as a guide to give very even spacing between rows of tucks. Once you have finished a row, place it in the groove that gives you the distance you desire and sew your next row.

Using a groove as a guide

Evenly spaced rows

Gathering Foot

As the name implies, a gathering foot is used to gather fabric. This category of foot can be divided into two main types. Some gathering feet only gather. Some gathering feet can simultaneously attach the gathered fabric to a flat piece. This foot does not pleat fabric, it gathers in a random manner.

Selection of gathering feet

GATHERING ONLY

This style of foot will gather only. It has no slot to accommodate a second layer of fabric.

Gathering only

Gathering Only Foot Anatomy

The underside of this foot has two levels. The front of the foot, which is lower, comes in contact with the feed dogs and feeds fabric positively until just before the needle. After the needle, the foot no longer touches the feed dogs and the fabric does not feed. This is what creates the gather.

Underside of foot

GATHERING AND ATTACHING

Some gathering feet are able to simultaneously attach the gathered fabric to the flat fabric. This can be a bit tricky, but when mastered it can be a time saver.

Gathering and Attaching Foot Anatomy

The underside of the sole is specially designed to put pressure on the fabric only in front of the needle. The fabric is fed firmly up to the needle. After the needle, there is no longer any pressure on the fabric, and the feed dogs no longer help the fabric feed. This causes the fabric to gather. There is a slot that accommodates the layer of fabric that the gathered layer is being attached to.

Underside of gathering feet

Looking at the foot from the front, you can see a slot. This slot holds a second layer of fabric and keeps it from gathering while it is being stitched.

Front of gathering feet with slot

USE THE RIGHT FOOT

It is important to know the maximum stitch width of your sewing machine as this will determine how far apart your feed dogs are. Gathering feet are available in different widths. If the gathering foot is too narrow, it might rest between the feed dogs and not feed fabric properly.

Narrow gathering foot resting between feed dogs

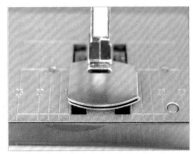

Wide gathering foot resting properly on feed dogs

A foot wider than the space between the feed dogs will work.

Narrow and wide gathering feet side by side

Narrow gathering foot resting properly on feed dogs

HOW TO ▶ Use a Gathering Foot for Gathering Only

The instructions for gathering only pertain both to the feet that gather only and to the feet that can gather and attach.

FABRICS MAKE A DIFFERENCE

Gathering is usually done with one layer of a fine fabric. Stiffer, heavier, or heavily starched fabrics do not gather well.

Fine fabrics can be easily pushed into the opening of a zigzag plate at the beginning of your stitching. In addition, gathering is often done near the edge of a piece of fabric, which can also cause the fabric to be pushed into the needle plate at the beginning of the seam. Using a straight-stitch needle plate can help minimize these problems.

SETTING UP THE MACHINE

It is a good idea to do a test sample with the fabric you are actually going to work with in your project. This can prevent frustration later on. Once the desired result is achieved, you can move forward with confidence.

1. Set your machine up as if you were doing a regular straight stitch at a stitch length of 2.5mm.

2. Set your top thread tension at its default setting. If your machine has a mechanical tension setting, this will be 4–4 ½" (10–11.5cm). If your machine has computerized tension, it will automatically go to default.

3. Remember to pull your thread through the needle opening of the presser foot.

4. Place your sample fabric under the presser foot and lower the foot.

5. Hold on to both top and bobbin threads for the first few stitches. Stitch until you can see how much the fabric is gathering.

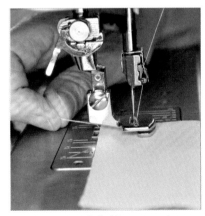

Beginning to stitch, holding top and bobbin threads

Adjusting the Amount of Gather

The amount of gather at default settings can vary greatly from machine to machine. By adjusting stitch length and top tension you can achieve your desired result.

Gathering at default settings on Shelley's machine

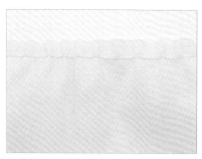

Gathering with longer, 4.5mm stitch length

Gathering with longer 4.5mm stitch length and increased upper tension at seven

Because the gathering is random, make sure you stitch a strip long enough to give you the desired end length.

DO A SAMPLE

Cut a 10" x 4" (25 × 10cm) strip of fabric. Gather as desired and measure the result. If it ends up at, for example, 5" (10cm), which is half of the original length, then you will know that you need a 40" (1m) strip to achieve a 20" (51cm) gathered strip. Doing measurements like this will help you determine the length of fabric you need for your project. This is just one example of measuring before and after. Your finished measurements may vary depending on the desired amount of gathering.

HOW TO Gather and Attach with a Gathering Foot

The two-tier versions of gathering feet, as well as being able to gather only as previously described, can simultaneously attach the gathered layer of fabric to a flat layer. Follow all the previous instructions to gather only on this style of foot.

POSITIONING THE TWO FABRICS

Position the fabric to be gathered between the foot and the feed dogs.

Slide the second piece of fabric into the slot of the presser foot.

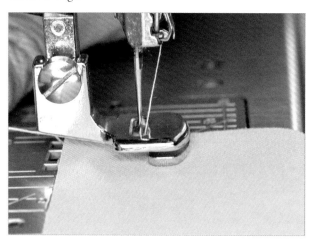

Positioning the fabric to be gathered

Second fabric in slot

THE FIRST STITCH IS IMPORTANT

Be sure that the needle can penetrate the fabrics on the first stitch. Once again, you will want to hang on to the top and bobbin thread when you begin stitching.

Beginning stitching

Guiding the two fabrics may take a little practice. Stitch slowly and let the machine feed the fabric. Guide the bottom fabric with one hand and the top fabric with the other. Most people will find it easiest to guide from in front of the foot.

Guiding fabrics

Gathered fabric stitched to non-gathered fabric

Patchwork Foot

You may wonder why we chose to pay so much attention to a foot that seems so simple. There are so many variations of this foot on the market that we often find that our students have bought the wrong one for their sewing machines. This has led to frustration for them and a feeling that they were doing something wrong when they did not get the result they were expecting.

The patchwork foot was designed to help sew a straight and accurate ¼" (6mm) seam. Some are designed to be used with the needle in center position. Others are used in conjunction with a stitch built into the machine that moves the needle to the right. Some have guides, and some do not.

Different styles of patchwork feet

TO GUIDE OR NOT TO GUIDE?

You might think that having a guide on your patchwork foot will make your piecing more accurate, and in some cases that might be true. However, in our classes we find that for some people, a guide can get in the way of accuracy.

Guides block your view of the fabric at the edge of the foot. Some are also quite flimsy. When these two elements are combined the result is usually a seam allowance that is too wide and finished blocks that measure too small. The reason for this is that the fabric pushes the guide to the right, increasing the distance from the edge of the fabric to the needle. Not all guides do this. If you consistently find your blocks too small, it may be worth looking at the guide as the culprit. In our classes we find ourselves removing guides for approximately half of our students.

Patchwork Foot Used with Needle in Center Position

All the feet in this section are designed to work with the needle set to center needle position. Your machine may allow you to make minor needle position adjustments to achieve better accuracy. For example, you may want to sew with a scant ¼" (6mm) seam allowance.

CENTER NEEDLE POSITION FOOT ANATOMY

The common denominator of the different styles of patchwork feet is that one or both side edges of the foot are ¼" (6mm) from the needle. The narrow opening between the toes combined with the flat bottom keep the fabric from flagging and help provide a balanced straight stitch as well as visibility.

Flat bottom

Patchwork Foot with Both Side Edges Equal Width from the Needle

This foot is appropriate for machines that have feed dogs set closer together. It is just wide enough to cover both long feed dogs. This ensures even and accurate feeding. These feet are available with and without guides. Some are also made with a slot to accommodate a Dual Feed/IDT mechanism.

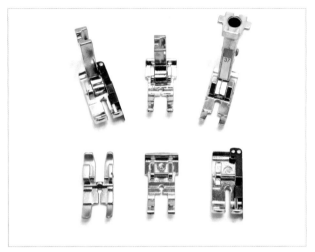

Patchwork feet with even side edges

EQUAL WIDTH SIDES FOOT ANATOMY

The most important feature of this foot is that the sole covers both feed dogs on the machines it was designed for. The needle is ¼" (6mm) from either side edge of this foot. Some have a ⅛" (3mm) measurement on the inside of the narrow toes. Most have markings to indicate where the needle penetrates fabric and ¼" (6mm) from beginning of fabric and ending of fabric. There may also be a marking for center needle position.

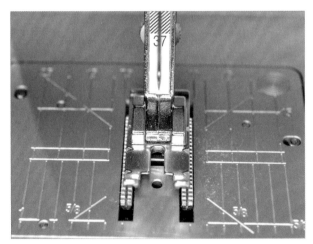

Sole covering both feed dogs

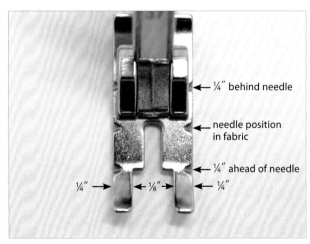

↤ ¼" behind needle

↤ needle position in fabric

↤ ¼" ahead of needle

¼" →   ↤ ⅛" →   ↤ ¼"

¼″ (6mm) and ⅛″ (3mm) seam allowance from both side edges

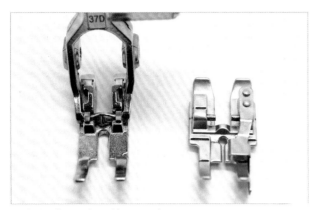

With slot for Dual Feed/IDT mechanism

Markings on feet

Patchwork Foot with Wider Left Side

To accommodate machines that have wider zigzag settings, this foot was designed to completely cover the left-side feed dog. This greatly improves fabric feeding. If you have a sewing machine that has wider (9mm) stitching, the narrower patchwork feet will sit between the feed dogs.

Wider patchwork feet

WIDER LEFT SIDE FOOT ANATOMY

The distance from the needle to the left side of this foot is greater to allow coverage of the left-side feed dog. This allows the fabric to feed more successfully. The ¼" (6mm) seam allowance is achieved on the right side of the foot. This foot may come with or without guides. It has markings to show needle insertion point and ¼" (6mm) before and after the needle. Depending on your machine, it may or may not have a slot for a Dual Feed/IDT mechanism.

Wider left side and markings

With and without slot for Dual Feed/IDT mechanism

USE THE PATCHWORK FOOT THAT MATCHES YOUR FEED DOGS

There are many machines that have wider zigzag settings, up to 9mm. This feature places the feed dogs farther apart. Patchwork feet designed for machines with a narrower maximum stitch width, for example, 5.5mm, will sit between the feed dogs, thus hindering the positive feeding of the fabric. As a result, the foot may not climb over seams evenly, and stitch length and seam allowances will be inconsistent.

Foot sitting between feed dogs

Coded Version Patchwork Foot

The coded version of this foot lets the machine know that it is using a patchwork foot. This information tells the machine to limit needle positions to fit inside the narrow opening of the foot, preventing damage from needle strikes.

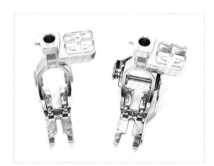

Coded patchwork feet

CODED VERSION PATCHWORK FOOT ANATOMY

The main feature in the anatomy of this foot is the lens that sends information back to the sewing machine. It is available in the narrow as well as wider versions in order to accommodate different feed dog spacings. It has markings for needle insertion and ¼˝ (6mm) in front of and behind the needle as well as a marking for center needle position. It may come with or without a guide. Some feet come with guides attached. One comes with a guide that attaches to the bed of the machine.

Lens on foot

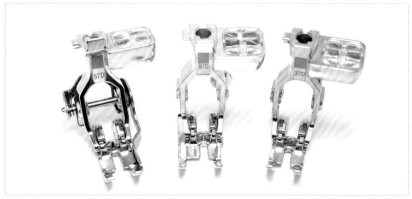

Wider and narrow versions

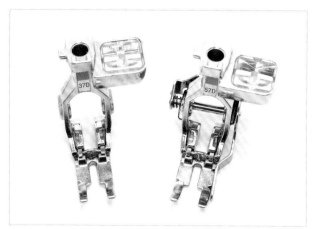

With and without guide

Guide that attaches to the bed of the machine

Patchwork Foot Used with Pre-Programmed Right Needle Position Stitch

The main feature of this type of foot is that the sole covers both feed dogs. There are a number of machines that have a straight stitch programmed to a right needle position for patchwork. These feet are designed to be used with that stitch.

Patchwork foot for right needle position stitch

PRE-PROGRAMMED NEEDLE POSITION STITCH FOOT ANATOMY

The opening in this foot is oriented to the right side and is large enough for a number of needle positions. This foot is available with or without a guide and has markings for needle insertion and ¼″ (6mm) before and after the needle. It may have a marking for ¼″ (6mm) to the left of the needle.

Patchwork feet with markings

Attach the presser foot to your machine. Select straight stitch or the ¼" (6mm) piecing stitch and set the length to approximately 2.0mm. This shorter stitch length helps prevent stitches from coming undone when subcutting at the beginning and end of the seam. Set the needle to stop in the down position if your machine has this capability. This stops the fabric from shifting accidentally if you stop.

Position the edge of the fabric to be sewn exactly along the right edge of the presser foot. Lower the foot and, holding on to the top and bobbin threads start sewing. After two or three stitches, let go of the two threads and continue to the end of the seam. The reason to hold on to the threads, is to prevent them from being pulled down into the machine and leaving a tangle.

Line up fabric with right edge of foot.

Hold threads and start sewing.

If you are using a foot with a guide, when you position the fabric, place it gently up against the guide, but don't push it against the guide as you sew. Too much pressure will push some guides to the right and increase the seam allowance. This will result in blocks that measure out small.

Fabric against guide

HEADERS AND FOOTERS

Headers and footers are a great idea to begin and end stitching. The header anchors top and bobbin threads, thus preventing them from bunching up under patchwork. For headers and footers, Shelley cuts 1" x 2" (2.5 × 5cm) rectangles of light-colored fabric and places them wrong sides together so she can enjoy the pretty side of the fabric as she sews.

Chain Piecing with Headers and Footers

Hold on to the top and bobbin threads and begin stitching onto a header. Stop with the needle down, one stitch off the edge of the header.

Stop with needle down one stitch off header.

Lift the presser foot and position the raw edge of the patchwork along the right edge of the presser foot, lining up the presser foot and raw edge of fabric exactly.

Position the fabric along the edge of the presser foot.

Stitch along the edge of the fabric, guiding with your fingers directly in front of the foot.

Fingers in front of foot

Sew to the end of the seam. Stop with the needle in the down position, one stitch beyond the bottom of the strip. Lift the presser foot and position the next strip. When you reach the end of the last piece, stop with the needle in the down position, one stitch off the end of the patchwork, raise the foot, and stitch onto a footer. Stop with the needle down, one stitch off the edge of the footer.

Trim threads between the footer and the last piece. The footer becomes the header when you begin stitching again. For more information see *Easy Precision Piecing* by Shelley Tobisch (C&T Publishing).

Stop with needle down, one stitch off edge of the footer.

Thread for Patchwork Feet

The best and most accurate results are achieved using a supple long staple Egyptian cotton thread. A 50-weight, 2-strand version like Aurifil or DMC are Shelley's go-to choices. There are certainly other good threads. Match or blend with background fabric.

Needle for Patchwork Feet

For Shelley's favorite threads, a size 70 HLX5 needle (by Organ Needle Company) or equivalent provides the best results. The sharp point of this needle is perfectly suited for quilting cottons.

Needle Position

The default needle position for the straight stitch you have selected is a good starting point. If your seam allowance is not accurate, you may want to adjust your needle position to the left or the right to fine-tune.

⚠ CAUTION

Patchwork feet have a very narrow opening for the needle. Moving the needle position too far may result in the needle hitting the foot.

Needle hitting foot   Needle damage on foot

Patchwork Troubleshooting

There are some things that may work against your accuracy when doing patchwork.

Needle Position and Presser Foot Alignment

If one or both of these settings are out of alignment, your accuracy will suffer. See Setting Up for Success, page 8. A visit to your friendly sewing machine technician may be in order.

Damaged Underside of Presser Foot

Often when chain piecing, sewists will leave a long gap between pieces. This allows the feed dogs to come into contact with the underside of the presser foot for an extended period of time. The metal of the feed dogs is usually harder than that of the presser foot. The sharp teeth can wear a series of grooves into the foot, which can create unevenness and roughness that can hamper the feeding of the fabric. It is a good idea to have a look underneath your ¼" foot and consider replacing it if there is a lot of damage.

Damaged underside of presser foot

Presser Foot Wobble

Some presser feet have a lot of side-to-side wobble. If this is excessive, you might find it hard to feed your patchwork accurately. It can sometimes be beneficial to use a foot that comes with a permanently attached shank and sole, as long as it lines up properly with the feed dogs and the center needle position.

Guiding Fabric from the Side of the Foot

This one may seem odd, but it can be a real game-changer. If you put your fingers lightly on the fabric in front of the presser foot, it will feed straighter. The moment you put your fingers to the side of the foot, it will try to sew in a circle. Try this for yourself and see what works for you.

Fingers in front of presser foot

Fingers at side of presser foot, fabric veers.

Presser Foot Pressure with Patchwork Feet

If you find the top layer of your fabric has increased in length when you get to the end of the seam, you may need to decrease the presser foot pressure; see Presser Foot Pressure (page 8).

EASY PRECISION PIECING
For more in-depth information on patchwork, see *Easy Precision Piecing* by Shelley Tobisch (C&T Publishing).

Embroidery and Appliqué Feet

This category of presser feet may be made of plastic, metal, or a combination of both. Most of them are open in the front for good visibility, but some are closed. They also come in coded, Dual Feed/IDT, and non-stick versions. The common feature is a hollow area on the underside of the foot to allow dense or bulky stitching to pass through. These feet are used with decorative and satin stitches, and the open-toe versions are an excellent choice for appliqué.

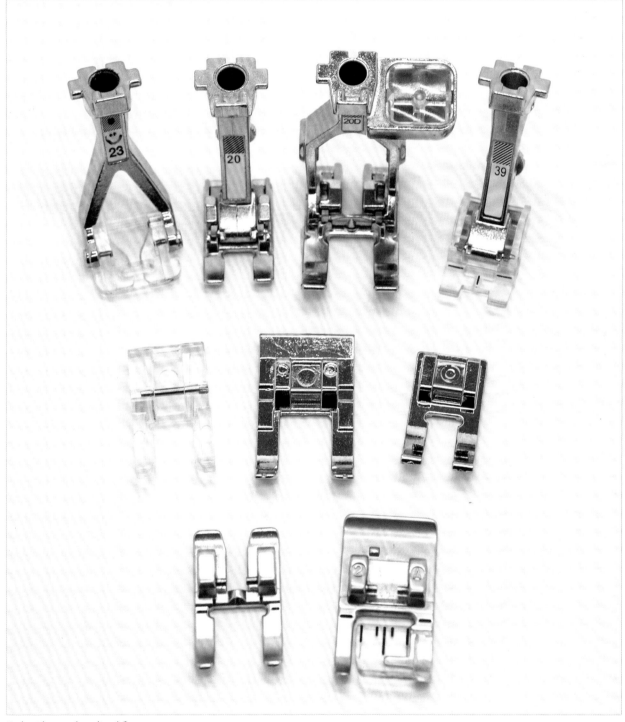

Embroidery and appliqué feet

Open-Toe Feet

The open-toe design of these feet provides an unobstructed view to the needle.

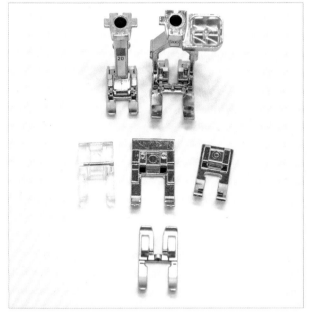

Open-toe feet

OPEN–TOE FOOT ANATOMY

Open-toe feet come in metal, plastic, or a combination of the two. The main feature is the hollow or groove in the underside of the foot to allow easy passage of dense, bulky stitching. This groove may be straight through or may be a V shape. The V shape allows for easier following of curved shapes.

Unobstructed view to the needle

Metal or plastic

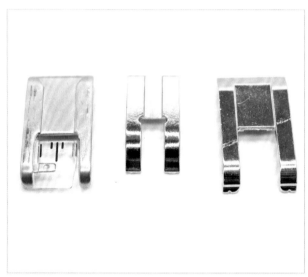

Underside of feet with straight-through groove

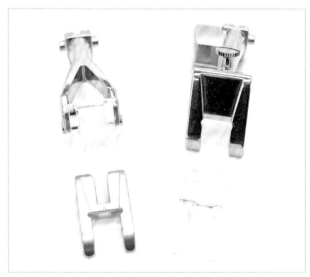

Underside of feet with V-shaped groove

Closed-Toe Feet

There are also closed-toe versions of these feet.

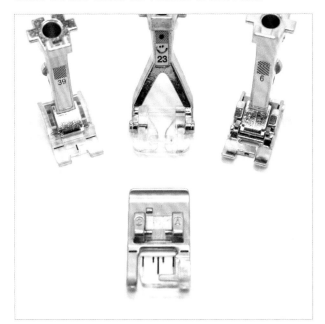

Closed-toe versions

CLOSED-TOE FOOT ANATOMY

The closed-toe versions of these feet are available in plastic or metal and have a bar in front of the needle location. This bar may have markings that act as a reference point for the position of the needle and placement of stitches. Some versions of these feet have a small hole in the front center of the bar to allow for the insertion and precise feeding of a fine cord into the stitching; see Single Fine Cord Foot (page 71). Clear versions of this foot offer good visibility.

Example of closed-toe embroidery foot

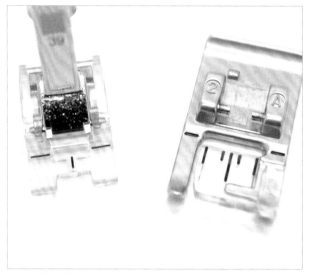

Feet with markings

Feet with opening for cord

Clear foot with narrow groove under bar

Attach your foot of choice.

DECORATIVE STITCHES

If the decorative stitch you intend to use has bulk (double and triple stitching), this foot is a good choice. The groove or channel will allow this bulk to pass through easily. Often, though, what makes the stitch attractive also causes it to tunnel the fabric. To overcome this problem, it is wise to stiffen or stabilize the fabric. This holds it firm and makes the difference between a beautiful row of stitching and one you will want to tear out.

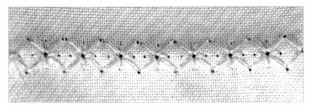

Tunneled decorative stitching

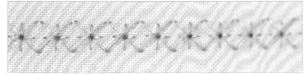

Stabilized and beautiful!

Tension for Decorative Stitches

Many recent sewing machines have automatic tensions that adjust to the stitch selected. Most models, though, don't have this feature. Decorative stitches are often done using specialty threads. The properties of these threads can make normal tension settings incorrect. This is true even if your machine has auto tension.

You may find that lowering your top tension slightly will improve your decorative stitching. If you are seeing a bit of bobbin thread at the outside edge of your stitches, then lower the setting until you can no longer see the bobbin thread. Do not lower it so far that the top thread loops on the underside of the fabric.

Needles for Decorative Stitches

Use a needle size that is appropriate for the thickness of the thread. The style or point should match the fabric you are working with; see Needles and Thread (page 12). There are specialty needles that work well with certain threads. Topstitch and metallic needles work better with metallic and monofilament threads by reducing the amount of friction in the eye.

Fabric Stiffeners

A fabric stiffener is a starch or starch-like product that adds body to your fabric. Shelley prefers to use this type of product as it does not add bulk to the row of stitching. Acorn Easy Press Fabric Treatment is her go-to.

Use Stabilizers

Where a fabric stiffener does not add enough body to prevent tunneling, you will need to use a stabilizer. Use the lightest stabilizer that will hold your stitches and fabric flat. Stabilizers are available as tearaway, washaway, and cutaway.

> ⚠ CAUTION
>
> Some tearaway stabilizers will distort the stitching when being torn away. Some cutaway stabilizers will add bulk to the edge of stitching if not cut close enough. It is a good idea to test a variety of stabilizers on samples before using them in your actual project.

APPLIQUÉ

To appliqué is to stitch a cut-out shape onto a larger piece of fabric. The shape may be turned, meaning the raw edges are turned under, or raw edge.

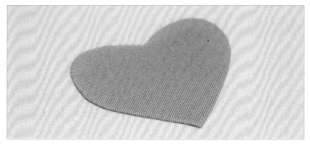

Turned-edge appliqué

Raw-edge appliqué

The stitches used for appliqué range from a simple zigzag to blanket stitch to mock hand appliqué.

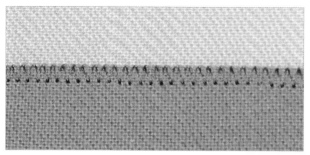

Zigzag appliqué

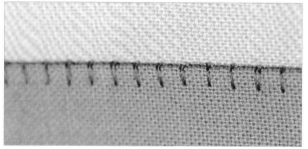

Blanket stitch appliqué

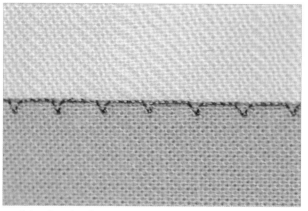

Mock hand appliqué

TIP

A knee-lift/free-hand system or hover feature (available on some computerized machines) is very handy for pivoting; see Knee-Lift/Free-Hand System (page 37). Be sure to select needle stop down.

Zigzag Stitch/Satin Stitch

Adjust your width and length, taking into consideration the size of the appliquéd shape. Do not overly shorten your stitch length as this may cause your fabric to stop feeding and your stitches to pile up. Keep the left side of the zigzag fully on the appliqué shape. Allow the right side to fall just off the edge of the appliqué shape into the background fabric. On an outside curve, pivot with the needle down in the background fabric. On an inside curve, pivot with the needle down, either in the appliqué shape or in the background fabric.

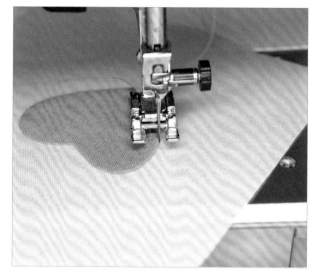

Zigzag stitch pivoting in background fabric on outside curve

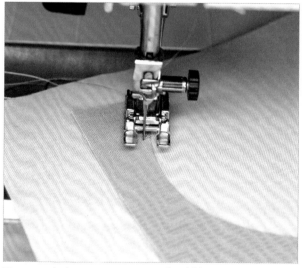

Zigzag stitch showing pivoting in appliqué fabric on inside curve

Blanket Stitch

Adjust width and length according to the size of the appliqué shape and the type of fabric being stitched around. For example, if working with a smooth cotton, the stitch may be shorter and narrower than that used for stitching a thicker fabric like flannel. If working with wool the stitch may be longer and wider. Keep the left swing of the needle fully on the appliqué shape. Allow the right swing to fall just off the edge of the appliqué shape. The straight-stitch portion of the stitch should follow exactly along the edge of the shape. Pivot only when the needle is in the background fabric.

Blanket stitch showing pivoting on background fabric

THE RIGHT STITCH MAKES A DIFFERENCE

A true blanket stitch for appliqué consists of one straight stitch forward, a stitch to the left, a stitch back to the right, and then forward again. There are no reverse stitches. Some machines only offer the blanket stitch with a reverse element. This makes sewing curves and turning corners more difficult and you may want to use a zigzag stitch instead. It's a good idea to test first.

Blanket Stitch Tension

Your thread choice may determine your top tension setting. You may find that lowering your top tension slightly will improve your stitching. If you are seeing a bit of bobbin thread at the outside edge of your appliqué, lower the setting until you can no longer see the bobbin thread. Do not lower it so far that the top thread loops on the underside of the fabric.

Thread Choice

Blanket-stitch appliqué can be done with anything from a very fine thread like WonderFil InvisaFil 100-weight and Quilters Select Para Cotton Poly 80-weight to a heavy Aurifil 12-weight Lana. The choices are endless.

Needles for Blanket Stitch

Use a needle in a size that is appropriate for the thickness of the thread, from a size 65/9 for the Quilters Select Para Cotton Poly to a size 110/18 for the Aurifil Lana. The style or point should match the fabric you are working with; see Needles and Thread (page 12).

Use Fabric Stiffeners

Adding extra body with a starch or starch-like product to the background fabric will help improve the quality of your stitches when stitching along the edge of the appliqué shape. For best results Shelley prefers Acorn Easy Press Fabric Treatment. Follow the manufacturer's instructions for your favorite product.

Try Stabilizers

Place stabilizer under the appliqué shape to support the fabric when working with dense stitching such as satin stitching. A stabilizer with short fibers that washes away, such as Quilters Select Print & Piece Fuse Lite, is a great choice.

MOCK HAND APPLIQUÉ

The mock hand appliqué stitch is used to mimic hand stitching. Many machines have this stitch built in. It is actually a mirror image of the blind hem stitch. In order to make this stitch nearly invisible it is important to adjust your length and width settings. A good place to start is a stitch length of 2.0mm and a width of 1.0mm. Adjust from there, making sure the needle just catches the folded edge of the fabric on its left swing. Pivot only when the needle is in the background fabric.

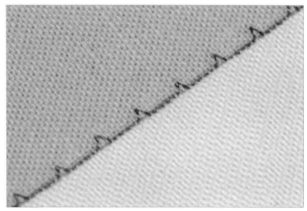

Mock hand appliqué

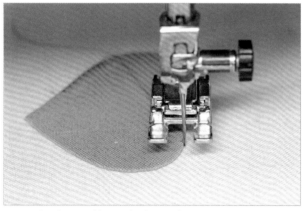

Pivot only when needle is in background.

Mock Hand Appliqué Tension

Your thread choice may determine your top tension setting. If you choose a monofilament thread for this technique, set your top tension to half of its normal default setting and fine-tune from there. For other threads start at default. If you are seeing a bit of bobbin thread at the outside edge of your appliqué, lower the setting until you can no longer see the bobbin thread. Do not lower it so far that the top thread loops on the underside of the fabric.

Thread Selection

For the best results this stitch is performed with an invisible thread on top and a fine cotton thread in the bobbin. Shelley's preferred choice is Superior Threads MonoPoly on top and Aurifil or DMC 50-weight cotton in the bobbin. If you prefer not to work with a monofilament, very fine threads give the next best results.

Needles for Mock Hand Appliqué

Use the finest needle that will accommodate the size of your thread; see Needles and Thread (page 12).

Try Fabric Stiffeners

Note that adding extra body with a starch or starch-like product to the background fabric will help improve the quality of your stitches when stitching along the edge of the appliqué shape. For best results Shelley prefers Acorn Easy Press Fabric Treatment. Follow the manufacturer's instructions for your favorite product.

Stabilizers

Place stabilizer under the appliqué shape to support the fabric when working with dense stitching such as satin stitching. A stabilizer with short fibers that washes away, such as Quilters Select Print & Piece Fuse Lite, is a great choice.

FOR FURTHER REFERENCE

For more in-depth information on machine appliqué, see some of Shelley's favorite, go-to machine appliqué books: *Alex Anderson's Hand & Machine Appliqué* by Alex Anderson, *Sewflakes: Papercut-Appliqué Quilts* by Kathy K. Wylie, *Mastering Machine Appliqué* by Harriet Hargrave, and *Stitching Classic Americana* by Masako Wakayama, all published by C&T Publishing.

Free-Motion or Darning Foot

Free-motion feet come in numerous styles. All are designed to allow the sewist to move the fabric freely in any desired direction rather than have the feed dogs move the fabric.

The variety of free-motion feet can be subdivided into two categories: feet that move up and down in synchronization with the needle and feet that are stationary.

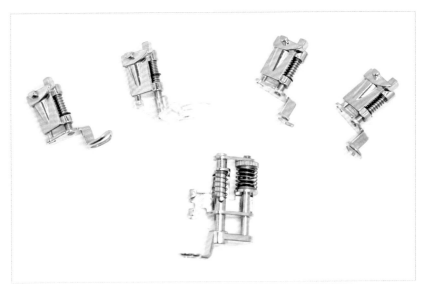

Variety of free-motion feet

Free-Motion Feet That Move up and Down

Many free-motion feet move up and down on the fabric in synchronization with the needle.

Feet that move up and down on the fabric

The foot lowers onto the fabric when the needle goes in. This keeps the fabric stable. As the stitch is formed, the needle lifts back out and the fabric is held down securely by the presser foot until the needle is well clear. This stops the needle from lifting the fabric, thereby preventing flagging.

Foot resting on fabric when the needle is in

Foot holding fabric down as needle lifts out of fabric

Foot lifted as needle is well clear

FREE-MOTION SPRING FOOT

One type of free-motion foot that moves up and down on the fabric is the free-motion spring foot.

Free-motion spring feet

Free-Motion Spring Foot Anatomy

The spring foot has a lever that sits above the machine's needle clamp. As the needle moves up and down, it raises and lowers the foot to assist in easier movement of the fabric and proper stitch formation. The foot has a spring that helps prevent flagging of the fabric as the needle is moving up.

Lever sitting on needle clamp

Needle clamp lifting foot

Needle clamp lowering foot

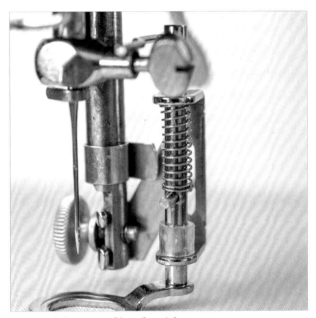
Spring to help prevent fabric from lifting

FREE-MOTION FEET WITH A HOPPER MECHANISM

Some sewing machines have a built-in mechanism that raises and lowers the presser foot in synchronization with the needle, thus eliminating the need for a lever over the needle clamp. This makes attaching the foot to the sewing machine quite easy.

Free-motion feet that work with a hopper mechanism

Hopper Mechanism Foot Anatomy

Feet that operate with a hopper mechanism have a spring that helps the foot adapt to the varying thicknesses of fabric and to prevent flagging.

A spring to prevent flagging

A VARIETY OF SOLES

One thing these different styles of free-motion feet have in common is that they come in a variety of sole types.

A variety of sole types

Small Sole Feet

One advantage of a foot with a smaller sole is that the fabric is supported closer to the needle, resulting in less flagging of the fabric as the needle lifts out. This helps prevent skipped stitches and frayed threads when doing free-motion work. These are available in straight-stitch and zigzag versions. The front may be open to offer greater visibility.

Small soles

⚠ CAUTION

It is possible that the sole with the front cutaway can get caught on thread basting and when crossing thicker seams.

Large Sole Feet

The large sole feet have an opening large enough to allow zigzag stitching. They generally offer good visibility.

Large soles

⚠ CAUTION

The larger the opening is in the sole of the foot, the more possibility there is for flagging.

Free-Motion Feet That Require the Presser Foot Lifter to Be Parked

There are machines that require the presser foot lifter to be in a certain position, part way down (or parked), in order for the free-motion foot to work properly.

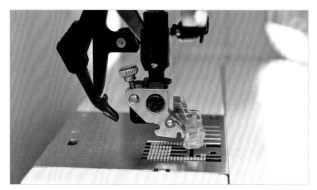

Foot that requires parking

PARKED PRESSER FOOT LIFTER FOOT ANATOMY

These feet come in in a variety of styles, including open and closed.

Parking the Foot

There is a ledge in the slot for the presser foot lifter lever. When using this style of free-motion foot, the presser foot lifter must sit on this ledge. If the foot is lowered all the way, it will not lift off of the fabric when the needle is up and it will be nearly impossible to move the fabric freely.

Ledge in presser foot lifter slot

Presser foot lifter resting on ledge

Correct position of foot over fabric when needle is up

Presser foot lowered incorrectly and not on ledge

Incorrect position of foot on fabric when needle is up

Free-Motion Feet That Stay Level

A number of free-motion feet do not move up and down on the fabric. Rather, they stay level and float at a height above the fabric.

Style of foot that stays level

One feature of these feet is that the height of the sole is adjustable to match the thickness of the fabric. There is also an anti-flagging spring.

Foot showing height-adjustment screw

⚠ CAUTION

If the foot is set too low, it can catch on the seams. If the foot is set too high, the fabric will flag.

Foot set too low

Foot set too high

Free-Motion Feet with Interchangeable Soles

Some manufacturers have created free-motion feet that come with a variety of soles. These may include closed, open, large plastic, and even ruler foot soles. The benefit of this style of foot is that the sole can be changed to suit the technique at hand and to the style that best suits you.

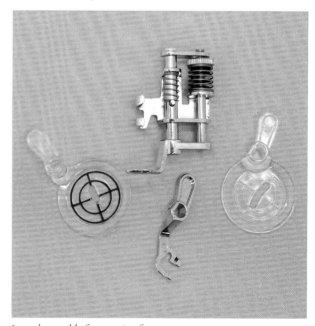

Interchangeable free-motion foot set

FREE-MOTION FOOT WITH INTERCHANGEABLE SOLES ANATOMY

The interchangeable soles are attached to the main portion of the foot by means of a screw.

Foot and sole separated

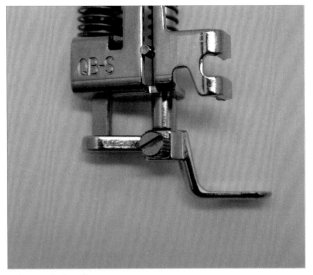

Sole attached to foot

HOW TO ▶ Use a Free-Motion Foot

STRAIGHTSTITCHING FREE-MOTION

1. Attach the foot as described in your machine manual.

2. Drop your feed dogs. If your machine does not allow you to do so, you may have a feed cover plate in your accessory kit. If not, set your stitch length to zero.

3. Set your machine to straight stitch.

4. Position the fabric and lower the foot.

5. Hold the top thread to the back and push the needle up/down button twice to do a complete stitch cycle. If your machine does not do this, turn the handwheel toward you for a complete stitch, stopping with the take-up lever at the top.

6. Pull up on the top thread and gently pull the bobbin thread up and out through the fabric. The reason for doing this is so that you can see where the bobbin thread is and not stitch it into the back of your fabric. If your machine has an automatic thread cutter, the bobbin thread will be too short to pull through, but it will also not leave a long thread on the underside. You may decide not to use the cutter when you are doing free-motion work.

Pull up bobbin thread.

7. Holding both threads, start stitching. Stop after a few stitches and cut off the long threads.

8. Resume sewing. Remember, it's you moving the fabric, not the feed dogs. It can be challenging at first to achieve an even stitch length. You will have to find a machine speed that you are comfortable with and then move the fabric faster for a longer stitch length or slower for a shorter stitch length.

Moving the fabric

PRACTICE!

The best thing you can do is practice, practice, and practice some more. It will come. Practice on pre-cut squares. Keep the side of the square that is closest to you parallel to the front of the machine. This will help you with control.

Keep the edge parallel to the front of the machine.

EASE YOUR WAY INTO FREE MOTION

There are a few things that will help you improve your free-motion stitching:

- Start at a medium speed. If your machine has a maximum speed control slide, set it where it is comfortable for you. Then, keep your foot to the floor.

- Practice by simply moving the fabric up, down, sideways, in circles, curves, or any way that feels good. Just get used to moving fabric.

- Go large. Make large curves and circles. This keeps them rounder. As you get better, you will find that you can work smaller and smaller.

- Wear quilter's gloves. They have rubberized fingertips. This enables you to put less downward pressure on the fabric, reducing friction.

ZIGZAG FREE-MOTION

Zigzag free-motion can be done with a free-motion foot that has an opening that allows you to zigzag. With this capability, you will be able to do monogramming and thread-painting techniques.

Follow the instructions for straightstitching, except set the machine to zigzag at a width that suits you.

Zigzag free-motion

You will want the machine to sew fast and to move the fabric slowly, so you can achieve a satin stitch.

Zigzag free-motion monogram

Walking Feet Versus Upper Feed Mechanisms

Walking foot and Dual Feed/IDT without foot attached

The walking foot and an upper feed mechanism (Dual Feed/IDT) are often perceived to give the same results. In fact, they are two different tools, designed to accomplish different sewing tasks well. Understanding the differences can be helpful.

How They Differ

WALKING FOOT

The feed dogs of the walking foot reach in front of the needle and help move fabric toward it. This helps to eliminate the top layer shifting that occurs when sewing, for example, fabrics with a layer of batting in between, fleeces, and other lofty fabrics. When stitching leather and vinyl, there is no friction from a presser foot sole while the fabric is being fed. This ensures a more even stitch length and positive feed. See How the Walking Foot Works, page 112.

Walking foot feed dogs reaching in front of needle

The walking foot is not designed for patchwork piecing. The ¼" (6mm) seam allowance used may mean that the right-side feed dogs do not engage with the fabric. This will allow the fabric to flag and may cause skipped stitches and degrade accuracy.

When machine quilting, the walking foot does a superb job of maintaining an even stitch length. Because of its design it will give beautiful pucker- and stretch-free stitching.

UPPER FEED MECHANISM

Dual Feed/IDT helps to feed fabric from behind the needle after it has already been sewn. It does not transport excess fabric to the needle. It does a beautiful job of maintaining an even stitch length and accurate fabric feeding on thinner or finer fabrics. However, because it cannot completely overcome the friction on the upper fabric at the front of the presser foot, when stitching on lofty fabrics such as fleeces and multi-layer

fabrics with batting, it may not fully eliminate the wave in front of the presser foot when sewing longer seams.

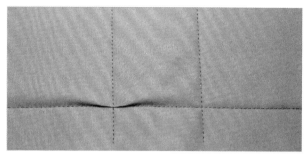

Comparison of seams with Dual Feed and walking foot

The seam on the left was sewn with Dual Feed/IDT mechanism, the one on the right with a walking foot.

The Dual Feed/IDT used with a ¼" foot does a superb job of patchwork piecing.

IN SHORT

A walking foot reaches in front of the needle to transport fabric, while a Dual Feed/IDT moves fabric from behind the needle that has already been stitched. This is a very important distinction and means that they are designed to accomplish different tasks.

Thankfully, there are machines available that will allow use of either a walking foot or upper feed mechanism depending on the task at hand.

Walking Foot

The walking foot, also known as even feed foot (not to be confused with Dual Feed or IDT), is an attachment which allows layers of otherwise difficult-to-feed fabric to move evenly under the foot. It helps to feed fabrics that have a tendency to shift and stretch the upper layer when sewing. Some examples might be fleece or high loft battings. It is also helpful when sewing leather or vinyl. These fabrics have a tendency to stick to the underside of a regular metal presser foot when the feed dogs are trying to move them.

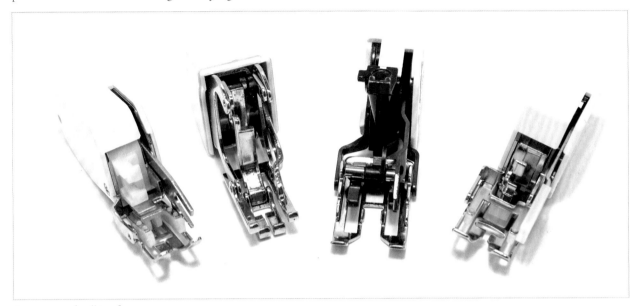

Assortment of walking feet

BUYING A WALKING FOOT

In our classes we often have students who have bought a walking foot that does not work well with their machine. For optimal performance, it is best to buy the brand and model of walking foot that is made specifically for your machine. This is important, because you want to match the feed dogs on the walking foot to the feed dogs of your sewing machine. This will ensure optimal feeding of your fabrics. If you choose to buy a generic version of a walking foot, your best results are always achieved if you can match the walking foot feed dogs to your machine's feed dogs. Higher quality will last longer and give better results. For example, some walking feet come with plastic tabs where they attach to the machine. These can break quite easily. The ones with metal attachment tabs last much longer and probably end up saving you money.

Plastic attachment tab

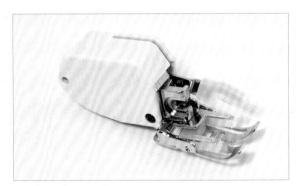

Metal attachment tab

Walking Foot Anatomy

The walking foot has a movable set of feed dogs. It has a lever that must be properly engaged to move these feed dogs up and down in synchronization with the machine's feed dogs and needle bar.

Upper feed dogs

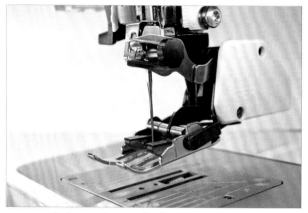

Lever attached to machine needle clamp

It also has a stationary sole that offers support while the needle is in the fabric. Many walking feet offer multiple soles to give the best result on a variety of tasks. These may include closed sole, open sole, and a sole with a center guide for edgestitching or stitching in the ditch. Most walking feet also include attachable seam guides.

Walking foot sole

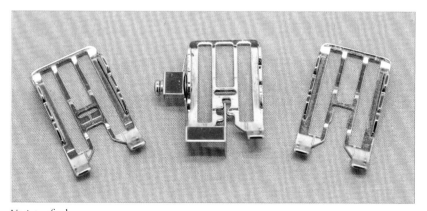

Variety of soles

Walking foot with seam guide attached

How the Walking Foot Works

Fabric is moved when the needle is up. Fabric is stationary when the needle is down. This is important to remember when learning how a walking foot works.

WHILE THE NEEDLE IS UP

Feeding occurs while the needle is out of the fabric and the lever is in the up position.

When the machine's feed dogs are moving the fabric, the feed dogs of the walking foot are down and in motion, holding the fabric securely and moving it along with the main feed dogs. The stationary sole is in the up position and not interfering with the fabric in any way.

Walking foot feed dogs moving fabric with machine feed dogs. Note: Stationary sole is in up position.

WHILE THE NEEDLE IS DOWN

When the needle and the lever are down, the stitch is being formed and the fabric is not being fed. At this time, the stationary sole of the walking foot is pressing firmly down on the fabric to hold it in place. The feed dogs of the walking foot are up and springing into their forward position, ready for the next feed cycle.

Stationary sole holding fabric down

Feed dogs up and forward

The feed dogs from the walking foot cannot actually move the fabric on their own. They are moved simply by the feed dogs on the sewing machine itself. This removes the friction that the underside of a regular presser foot creates and stops the top layer from stretching.

When machine quilting, there are two layers of fabric with batting in between. The loft of the batting, combined with the friction created by the underside of a regular presser foot, causes the top layer of fabric to stretch and shift. This creates a wave in front of the presser foot. As this wave approaches a cross-seam, it will create a fold. Using a walking foot solves this problem.

Approaching cross-seam

Fold over cross-seam

Because the walking foot feed dogs reach in front of the needle to transport fabric, they can help eliminate the bow wave that is created when feeding soft, lofty layers.

Top layer not stretched using walking foot, no bow wave

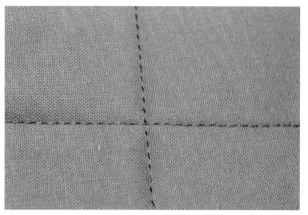

No fold over cross-seam using walking foot

USE A WALKING FOOT FOR SPECIALTY FABRICS

Not just for quilting, a walking foot is also helpful when working with materials such as leather and vinyl, which tend to stick to the underside of a regular presser foot. Because the stationary sole is only on the fabric during the non-feeding portion of the stitch cycle, there is no friction to hold back these sticky fabrics. Sometimes, sewing stretchy materials such as Lycra, fleece, and rib knits can be easier using this foot. It can also be helpful when matching plaids and stripes.

Stretchy fabrics sewn without a walking foot, top fabric stretched. Top fabric is shown on bottom to show the effect

Stretchy fabrics sewn with a walking foot, top fabric not stretched

WILL IT WORK IN REVERSE?

Most walking feet can be used with zigzag and forward and reverse decorative stitches.

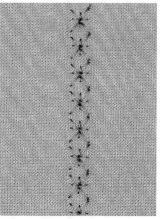

Walking foot with decorative stitch on fabrics with batting in between

It's pretty easy to use a walking foot. Problems do arise when they are not attached properly.

ATTACHING THE WALKING FOOT PROPERLY

Screw-on Type

Different manufacturers have different ways to attach the walking foot. The most common is to remove the entire presser foot and shank from the presser bar of the sewing machine. This usually means removing the screw that holds the shank in place. On some machines you may get away with just loosening the screw.

Removing screw

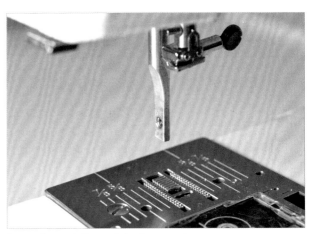

Presser bar with foot and shank removed

The walking foot is then attached where the shank was attached. In some cases, the manufacturer provides a slightly longer screw with the walking foot. It is important at this point to ensure that the lever is engaged properly either on or above the needle clamp, depending on the style of walking foot. If your sewing machine has a higher presser foot lift setting, this is a great time to use it.

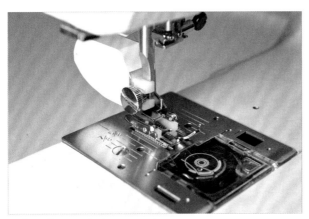

Walking foot attached to presser bar

Lever attached to needle clamp

Clamp-on Style

Another style of walking foot attachment is the clamp-on version. The easiest way to attach this type is to first slip the forked lever onto the needle clamp. Then, insert the cone into the opening of the foot and clamp it in place. This can be made easier by temporarily lowering the sewing machine's feed dogs, giving you more room to work. The presser bar can be lifted higher by using the machine's knee lift.

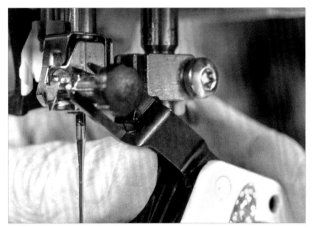

Forked lever on needle clamp

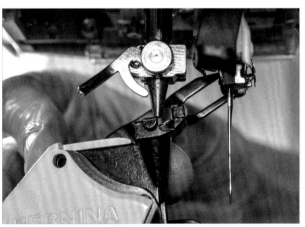

Inserting cone

Clamping foot in place

For both styles of these walking feet, you will know they are attached properly when the feed dogs of the walking foot move up and down as the needle bar moves. When the lever is up, the feed dogs are down. When the lever is down, the feed dogs are up.

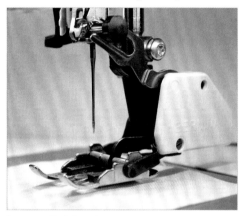

Lever up, feed dogs down

Lever down, feed dogs up

⚠ CAUTION

If you forget to put the lever on the walking foot in its proper position, either on or above the needle clamp, you will find that your fabric does not feed. If you need to pull on your fabric, it is a sign to check the lever position.

It is also very possible that you may damage the walking foot. The needle clamp, as it crashes down on top of the disengaged walking foot lever, can bend or break not just the lever but also the foot. In some cases, it may damage the needle clamp.

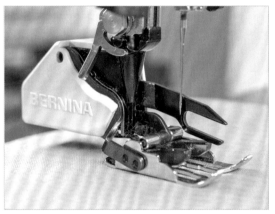

Lever not attached properly

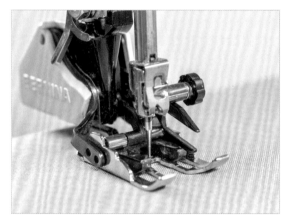

Needle clamp striking lever

CHANGING SOLES

Changing soles is pretty straightforward. Turn the silver screw on the side of the walking foot in a counterclockwise direction. This will separate the two black metal pieces that hold the sole in place. When the sole is loose, remove it and insert the desired one. Retighten the silver screw.

Note: Just loosen the silver screw. Do not try to remove it.

Servicing Your Clamp-on Walking Foot

Benefits of the clamp-on style of walking foot are its longevity and that it can be serviced. When your fabric no longer feeds properly, it may be time for some maintenance. Applying a drop of oil to each of the pivot points and working it in by moving the lever will have your fabric feeding again in no time. It is also possible that a spring inside has become dislodged. You can easily reattach this. With proper care this walking foot can last as long as your machine.

Most walking feet on the market are disposable. When they stop working, you just buy a new one. One has been made to last a long time—as far as I know, the BERNINA walking foot is the only one that can be serviced in a few easy steps to keep it running smoothly and last even longer. A sign that service is needed is that stitch length is uneven or the fabric has puckers.

1. Lift the white plastic cover over the silver screw and slide it off completely. **A**

2. Remove the two screws, as indicated by the pointers. **B**

3. Put a drop of sewing machine oil at the pivot, as shown by the pointer. Check to see that the springs are hooked up as they are in the photo. **C**

4. Gently pull out the forked lever and oil where indicated by pointers. **D**

5. Check that the silver bearings are turning freely; if they are not, the arm they are on may be slightly bent. Make sure they are perfectly horizontal to the walking foot body. Bend them back gently if needed. If you are worried about doing this, take the walking foot in to the dealer and have them service it. Put a small amount of oil on the shaft of the bearings and on top of the feed dogs they rest on. Wipe off any excess—you don't want it on your fabric. **E**

6. Turn the walking foot upside down and inspect the rubber feed dogs. If there are chunks missing or grooves worn into them, they can be replaced by your dealer. **F**

7. Reassemble in reverse order.

A. Lift the plastic cover.

B. Remove screws.

C. Oil at the pivot.

D. Pull out lever.

E. Check bearings.

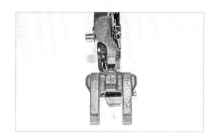

F. Inspect rubber feed dogs.

Permanently Attached Upper Feed Dogs

Your machine may have upper feed dogs that are permanently attached and disengageable. The feed dogs are lowered when needed and raised out of the way when not.

To use these feed dogs, you will have to attach the appropriate presser foot for your task.

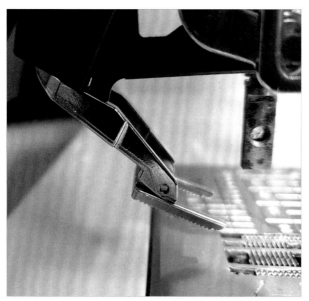

Permanently attached upper feed dogs

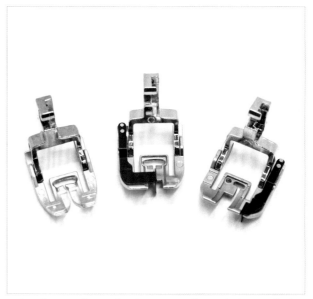

Styles of presser feet used with permanently attached upper feed dogs

To attach the presser foot, first remove the foot and shank on the machine. Attach the desired foot for the upper feed dogs, the same way you would attach the regular shank.

Hook-in Upper Feed Dogs Style Walking Foot

There are versions of the walking foot that hook into a bar at the back of the machine above the presser bar area.

There are a number of soles available for this style of walking foot.

Hook-in upper feed dogs, wide and narrow

Various soles available

A plastic clip on either side of the foot clips on to a metal tab on the sole. This makes it easy to change styles. Just pull straight out and replace by pushing the metal tabs into the plastic clip.

Foot showing plastic clips

Sole with metal tab

Slide metal tab into plastic clip.

To attach the foot to the machine, first remove the presser foot and shank. Slip the silver metal hook of the walking foot onto the bar at the back of the machine. Screw the shank onto the presser bar.

Hook in at the back of machine.

Screw foot onto presser bar.

Upper Feed Mechanism (Dual Feed or IDT)

An upper feed mechanism, available on many machines today, helps to feed two layers of fabric evenly. Depending on the manufacturer, it may be called Dual Feed or IDT (Independent Dual Transport).

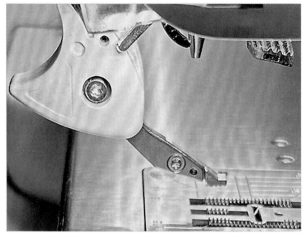

Dual Feed mechanism

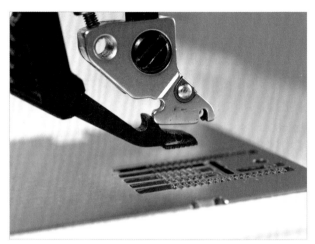

Independent Dual Transport

When sewing two long strips of fabric together, this feature helps to minimize the shifting of the top layer. This ability makes it very useful for accurate piecing and matching plaids and stripes. It helps maintain an even stitch length sewing over seams. Because it is built into the machine, it can be engaged or disengaged as needed. When engaged, it works with specially designed feet that have a slot built in to accommodate the feet.

Stripes sewn without upper feed mechanism

Stripes sewn with upper feed mechanism

Upper Feed Mechanism Foot Anatomy

The Dual Feed mechanism is positioned at the back of the presser bar. When engaged, the toe sits in a slot in the back of the presser foot being used. This toe sits on top of the center block of the feed dogs and moves in synchronization.

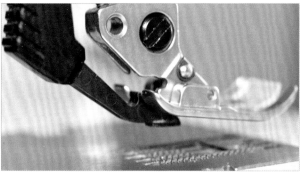

Upper feed mechanism engaged with foot

Upper feed mechanism engaged without presser foot, sitting on center block of feed dogs

IS IT WORKING PROPERLY?

With time, the position of the IDT on the center block of the feed dogs may change. This will affect feeding. An adjustment can be made by your sewing machine technician to correct this.

Proper position of upper feed mechanism

Misaligned upper feed mechanism

ENGAGING AND DISENGAGING DUAL FEED

With the presser foot in the up position, a downward and slightly forward push in the right spot will engage the Dual Feed. The toe will fit into a slot in the back of the presser foot being used.

Engaging Dual Feed mechanism

Engaging Independent Dual Transport

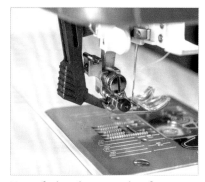

Upper feed mechanism in slot of presser foot

Be sure to use only presser feet that are designed to accommodate the upper feed mechanism. These feet will have a slot in the back to accommodate the upper feed dog.

Foot with slot in back

Wrong presser foot with no slot

To disengage the Dual Feed, move the presser foot to the up position. Use a downward push and slight pull back on the Dual Feed. This will allow a spring to pull the upper feed mechanism into its disengaged position.

HOW TO ▸ Use Upper Feed Mechanism

There are a number of specialty feet that work with a Dual Feed/IDT mechanism. For instructions on using those specialty feet, refer to the how-to section for the foot you would like to use.

If you start your seam with the upper feed mechanism off the fabric, it is possible that it may slide underneath the fabric. This can create a fabric jam at the beginning of your seam. To prevent this issue, keep an eye on your fabric at the beginning of the seam to make sure it stays under the upper feed mechanism.

Fabric caught on upper feed mechanism at beginning of seam

Index

U

V

W

Z

About the Authors

SHELLEY discovered the joy of quilting 37 years ago and has been sharing her love for it ever since.

BERNIE has been a sewing machine technician for all brands for 48 years.

Together they have taught as a team for 30 years. Shelley and Bernie have gained even more followers as course instructors on the innovative and interactive platform Creative Spark Online Learning (by C&T Publishing).

*Visit Shelley and Bernie online
and follow on social media!*

WEBSITE: easyprecisionpiecing.com

INSTAGRAM: @shelleyscott_tobisch and @bernietobisch

CREATIVE SPARK: creativespark.ctpub.com

CREATIVE
SPARK
ONLINE LEARNING

Crafty courses to become an expert maker..

From their studio to yours, Creative Spark instructors are teaching you how to create and become a master of your craft. So not only do you get a look inside their creative space, you also get to be a part of engaging courses that would typically be a one or multi-day workshop from the comfort of your home.

Creative Spark is not your one-size-fits-all online learning experience. We welcome you to be who you are, share, create, and belong.

Scan for a gift from u

creativespark.ctpub.com